# OUR CHURCH TODAY

## What It Is and Can Be

### G. Arthur Keough

Review and Herald Publishing Association
Nashville, TN          Washington, DC

Copyright © 1980 by
Review and Herald Publishing Association
Published in Nashville, Tennessee

This book was
Edited by Richard W. Coffen
Designed by Mark O'Connor

Type set: 10/11 Times Roman

Printed in U.S.A.


**Library of Congress Cataloging in Publication Data**

Keough, G Arthur, 1909-
    Our church today.

    Includes bibliographical references.
    1. Church.    2. Seventh-day Adventists—Doctrinal
and controversial works—Seventh-day Adventist authors.
I. Title.
BV600.2.K42        230'.67        80-19816
ISBN: 0-8127-0300-6

# Contents

# Dedication

To all those who would like to see the church
Rise to its responsibilities
And fulfill its mission
In the world today

# Preface

The purpose of this book is to introduce the reader to the real meaning of the church.

The writer believes that the church can be criticized and, if need be, corrected only as men and women, both inside and outside its circle, understand what the church stands for and its true nature. Only when members of the church perceive the essence of the church, rather than its external patterns, can they enable it to fulfill its function in the world today.

There is no dearth in the market of books on the church, and the writer has consulted many of them in writing this book. But every writer has his own bias and a particular emphasis that he makes. In this sense no book duplicates what another has written. This book is written with the purpose of presenting what a Seventh-day Adventist considers important in the church.

Where shall we go for authoritative material about the church? The obvious major source is the Bible. Despite the growth and development of the church down through the centuries, the Bible reveals the principles to which the church must ever be true. Although Scripture does not describe every possible facet of the church today, it lays down principles from which the church dare never deviate.

In quoting from the Bible the writer has decided to use the New International Version.* Other English versions give important insights regarding the message of the original languages of the Bible. But we will stay with the New International Version in order to maintain a uniformity in reference to what Scripture says.

The writer recognizes that he has used the masculine noun and

---

* Copyright © 1973, 1978 by The New York International Bible Society and is used by permission.

pronoun when referring to the church member. He hopes the stalwart women in the church will forgive him and recognize that he has done so with the generic sense of the masculine in mind. It seemed to savor of pedantry to say "he or she" all the time!

Finally, it may be important to point out that the writer holds a conservative view of the Bible as the Word of God. Labels are very difficult to use with any exactness of meaning. The term *conservative* may not mean very much at this point, but the reader will soon find that the writer accepts the Biblical statements as authentic and authoritative. He seeks to understand what is written, without raising questions of interest to the higher critic.

This conservative stance will doubtless color the concept of the church as it is presented. But it is only fair to the reader to let him know the presuppositions that underlie the writer's conclusions. In this way he can be forewarned or encouraged to proceed with reading the book.

The writer hopes and prays that a careful study of what the church is and ought to be will make its members stronger in their faith and better able to contribute to the betterment of the church. The goal is a presence of the church in the world that will lead it to fulfill its mission gloriously. At the same time it will hopefully dull the knife-edge of criticism from the outside that often is ill-advised and unfair.

# Introduction

In recent years the church has come under severe criticism. Many feel that its teachings are no longer acceptable in a scientific age; that its ritual and symbolism are meaningless and antiquated; that its programs, social and political, are ineffective; that its spiritual influence on the community is minimal. Some go so far as to say that although the church served well in the past and needs respect for the contribution it has made to civilization, now it no longer serves a useful purpose.

Those inside and outside the church have voiced this criticism. As a result many have stopped going to church. Others go once a year—at Easter time—or once in a lifetime—at marriage. Church congregations have dwindled to a very few, and church buildings have had to be sold for other purposes. Some churches still vie with social institutions, but for the most part they come out worse.

How do you feel about your church? Would you like to see a change in leadership? in organization? Would you like to modify its doctrines or perhaps establish a creed? Do you find the service cold and formal? Do you question the conversion of the members? Do you feel that many may be "honest to God" but in their daily lives are not honest with their fellowmen?

Two important questions need to be raised:

1. Should the church be criticized at all?

Some would say that the church is beyond criticism. They believe that to criticize it is to lay oneself open to condemnation by the authority vested in the church.

Much can be said for such hesitation. We should recognize that criticism is a serious undertaking. We must not engage in it lightly. Yet to consider the church beyond the pale of questioning puts it on a pedestal, and such a church may become arbitrary and intolerable. Reformation always springs from valid criticism, and reformation is important in the church, considering its human situation.

2. On what basis should criticism be leveled at the church, if at all?

To criticize the church because it does not meet *our* particular desires, *our* standards of teaching or conduct, *our* preferences in organization or policy, is to engage in a purely subjective exercise. It makes the church a reflection of ourselves, and thus it becomes as changeable and fickle as we are. No one would accept such a standard, although I am afraid that many who criticize the church do not distinguish between principle and personal prejudice.

Any criticism of the church must be based on what it is or ought to be. The church must be true to its nature, to the reason for which Christ established it. Only when it deviates from its charter should it be criticized and reformed.

This principle demands that we study and understand the church as it really is. It is the thesis of this book that the church is more than a social phenomenon. It is more than a group of men and women with common interests meeting together to serve their common ends. It represents God's activity in the world and man's response to that activity in grateful acquiescence and willing obedience.

If we look at the word *church,* we are impressed with the fact that it comes from the German *Kirche* and ultimately from a Greek word, *kuriakos,* meaning "belonging to the Lord."

If we look at another word in English related to the activity of the church—*ecclesiastical*—we find that its etymology leads to the Greek word *ekklēsia,* which the Greeks used to refer to an assembly or a people "called out."

Thus the very terminology of the church leads us to the concept of that which has a lord, that which has been called out for a specific purpose.

Every church has a history. Are you acquainted with the history of your church? Do you know where it has come from? what its traditions are? how and when it was established? These questions need answering if we wish to be adequately informed about our church.

In the following pages we look for the origin of the church in the Bible. We see that man is not left to his own devices. God is in control. He was in control not only before man sinned but also after the Fall. God has His plans and purposes that He is seeking to work out in and through man. Sometimes it seems that the forces of evil have gained control. As long as God permits individuals to make their own choices, there will be those who choose to do evil. But in the midst of evil God has a church composed of those who acknowledge His greatness and goodness and who stand as a testimony to God's saving power.

Because the church represents God's activity, it is based on firm foundations. Like the house built upon a rock, it will withstand all the buffetings that come against it. God who has begun a good work will finish it.

Although the church is God's institution, it walks on human feet. This is both its strength and its weakness. But it has clear distinguishing marks, and we shall try to define them. For it is important to differentiate the true from the spurious.

Since the church is human and divine, there will be an interplay of relationships. The Bible uses many meaningful metaphors, because no single human relationship can fully comprehend all that is involved in the interaction between a man and his God.

Two contrasts in the church are ever present: the call to holiness and the shadow of sin. We must look at these so that we can understand God's purposes and the human situation. Furthermore, we must recognize that unity and perfection are possible only in Christ.

There follows, therefore, an ever present need for discipline, both to maintain the purity of witness and to pursue the primary function of the church of reaching out to others. For the church does not exist to bolster its own ego but to serve others.

To meet this purpose the church needs to be organized for efficiency, and its leaders must recognize that their duty is not so much to rule as to serve. Only as servants can they truly follow the example of their Lord.

Finally, the church looks forward to a consummation of all things, to a time when sin and sinners will be destroyed and when Christ's kingdom will be established forever. Church members must prepare for that event. With hands on the plow today, their eyes focus on the goal of their endeavor—the establishment of Christ's kingdom of peace.

The writer hopes and prays that this book will make your church and mine a more meaningful organization in the world today and will enable each one to make the kind of contribution that will extend God's rule on the earth.

Chapter 1

# God in Control

The Bible makes it clear that God is in control of the universe. In fact, the Bible begins with God. It points out that if we want to seek for origins, we do not look to chance explosions of stars or to a favorable locus for life to develop. We look to a personal God who "spoke, and it came to be; he commanded, and it stood firm." [1]

Faith in the Biblical revelation enables the Christian to be sure of origins. The writer to the Hebrews says, "By faith we understand that the universe was formed at God's command, so that what is seen was not made out of what was visible." [2] He defines faith as "being sure of what we hope for and certain of what we do not see." [3] He adds that "this is what the ancients were commended for." [4]

The Christian thus stands in line with those down through the ages who have pinned their faith on the God who has created the universe. They believe that we have in Scripture a record of a God who has communicated with man and that this communication is dependable. When the speculations of man conflict with what God has revealed, he accepts the latter as true.

The Bible teaches us authoritatively about origins. In it we learn that everything God created was good, indeed, very good. [5] When we look at the intricacies of nature, we cannot help but marvel at the beauty of form and structure, the delicate interrelationship of the various parts. We are struck with the planning that must have gone on behind it and with the infinite greatness of the One who masterminded it. David, contemplating his birth and being, was able to say, "I am fearfully and wonderfully made." The Christian today, with the vast increase in knowledge, can say to God along with the psalmist and with greater understanding, "Your works are wonderful, I know that full well." [6]

Yet anyone looking at nature can see that much in the world is

far from beautiful. Sickness and disease, pain and suffering, death
and death-dealing, are all around him. Why are men selfish and
cruel? Why are hurricanes allowed to do so much damage? Is God
good when He permits such things? Is God in control, or is man
subject to his environment?

These questions raise important issues. Fortunately for us the
Bible lays down principles that help us understand what is happening and why. To the Bible, therefore, we turn for the answers to our
questions.

### Freedom to Be Wrong

God in His infinite love and wisdom created persons who were
perfect and free—free to be wrong if they wanted that! The alternative was to create automatons. But if God had created a universe
full of creatures who could do nothing but what they were pro-
grammed to do, then indeed the universe would be a large piece of
clockwork. It might be a wonderful piece of machinery, but it
would not be much more than that. It is to the glory of God that He
created beings who were free to worship Him with mind and will,
for thus their worship can be meaningful.

But in granting freedom of choice, God undertook a tremendous risk. There would always be the possibility that someone
would choose to pursue a course that God in His infinite wisdom
and love had not laid down. In such a case there would be a conflict
between truth and error. Since God is a God of truth and since only
truth can be established forever, error would have to be annihilated.

Such a conflict did arise in the universe, and it began with a
being closest to the throne of God!

Two passages of Scripture paint the picture for us: Isaiah
14:12-15 and Ezekiel 28:12-19. The first is set in the context of a
prophecy against Babylon, and the second is set in the context of a
prophecy against the king of Tyre. A study of both passages
indicates that the prophets referred to something that transcends the
human situation.

Let us look at the picture the prophets drew and at the issues
involved.

The being is addressed as "morning star, son of the dawn" and
is said to have "fallen from heaven" and to "have been cast down
to the earth." [7] He is described as "the model of perfection, full of

wisdom and perfect in beauty'' and was adorned with every precious stone. He was "anointed as a guardian cherub" and was "blameless" in all his ways.[8]

The sin that brought the being's downfall was pride. He said, "I will make myself like the Most High."[9] In desiring to be like the Most High he did not seek to be like Him in character but only in power and position. Apparently he did not realize that God's attributes are the basis of His power and that power without goodness is tyranny. Or if he realized this, he refused to recognize it, and by the choice he made he threw himself into opposition with God.

In this way, according to the Bible, sin and rebellion entered the universe, and it has been the source of all our woe. John the revelator saw the conflict in heaven between the two protagonists and the consequences of the struggle. "And there was war in heaven. Michael and his angels fought against the dragon, and the dragon and his angels fought back. But he was not strong enough, and they lost their place in heaven. The great dragon was hurled down—that ancient serpent called the devil or Satan, who leads the whole world astray. He was hurled to the earth, and his angels with him."[10]

The defeat of rebellion meant that God was in control, but it also meant that a new element had entered the universe, one that would have to be handled with infinite wisdom.

### Choosing to Sin

The second tragedy took place in the Garden of Eden. Our first parents, created in God's image, decided that they would disobey God's command. They thus placed themselves on the side of rebellion.

How could they do this? Most of us would say that if we were in their position, we would not be guilty of such a deed. But in so saying we would be ignoring the subtlety of sin. Apart from complete trust in God and His revelation we are all prone to fall.

We do not know all the thoughts that coursed through the minds of our first parents as they faced temptation and as they made their decisions. Eve admitted that she had been deceived.[11] Adam was not deceived but made a deliberate choice.[12]

An important point to note is that the sin was not merely partaking of the fruit from the forbidden tree. The sin lay in the acceptance of the imputation that God was not fair or loving in the restriction that He had made in the Garden of Eden. It involved believing the suggestion that though God was generous in providing the fruit of all the other trees, He was stingy in preventing access to the most important tree, the one that would lead to greatness and glory. The acceptance of this allegation against the character of God constituted the sin.

Our first parents apparently did not realize that all true freedom involves restriction. The football player must play according to the rules of the game, or he cannot continue to play. The athlete must observe the rules of the contest in which he is engaged, or he cannot win the prize. Only when we all obey the rules of the road can traffic move along swiftly and efficiently. Only when the laws of the land are honored and accepted can there be peace and prosperity.

The acceptance of God's order underlies all happiness. But it is easy to be wise after the event. The truth to notice is that God has left the door open to sin. If a person wishes to do wrong, he can do so. But he can do so only as he denies God's true character and motives. Because he denies what ought to be clear and obvious, he deserves the consequences of his act—eternal separation from God.

Was God in control in the Garden of Eden? Yes, He was. Not in the sense that He dictated every move. Rather He was perfectly fair in indicating mankind's duties and responsibilities and in issuing warnings, so that man in his freedom would be responsible for his actions.

### Response to Sin

An important truth taught in the Bible is that God is never caught unawares. He knows the end from the beginning.[13] Because of this truth many people ask such questions as: If God knew that the guardian cherub would sin in heaven, why did He create him? If God knew that Adam and Eve would eat the fruit of the forbidden tree, why did He place the tree in the Garden of Eden? Why does not God prevent evil?

All these questions contain the suggestion that God should control everything so that nothing untoward would happen. But if God did this, there would be an end to freedom. His creatures would worship Him only because they were conditioned to do so. Such a universe would be intolerable to the God whom we know by revelation. The only way to have a perfect universe is for God to grant individual freedom and for God to rule on the basis of love and understanding.

God's response to sin was to prevent man from eating of the tree of life and thus becoming eternal sinners.[14] God cannot condone sin in any part of His universe.[15] But God's graciousness was revealed in that He had already made provision for man's redemption. Man would have to suffer the consequences of his sin—but in a partial sense. However, if he realigned himself with God and repudiated the false concepts he had held, he could be restored to sonship and communion with God.

God's reaction to man's sin must have come as a surprise to our first parents. They knew that they could expect only death, yet God had given them a new lease on life, an opportunity for them to repent. They had lost the clothing of light that they had had before the Fall. Now they were conscious of their nakedness, but God provided them with furs, a much more fitting covering than fig leaves. God had come seeking them and had not waited for them to seek Him. And when He had questioned them, He had permitted them to defend themselves, if they could. This was an entirely different kind of God from the one portrayed by the serpent. I imagine they were thoroughly chagrined.

But the best news came with the announcement that there would be enmity between the offspring of the woman and the offspring of the serpent. As a result the serpent's head would be crushed.[16] Here was hope that would make everything else comparatively easy to bear. We do not know how much of the gospel our first parents understood. The record of what happened in the Garden is brief. But we may be sure that they gratefully accepted God's provisions, and we expect to see them in God's kingdom.

In this part of the story of Adam and Eve we see God not only in control but in gracious control. Where sin increases, grace increases even more.[17]

## People and Prophets

The Old Testament records God's dealings with His people from the time of Adam and Eve to Malachi, the last of the prophets.

Throughout, there is clear indication that God directed and warned, punished and restored. Do we find God in control?

If we think of control in the sense of exercising initiative and pursuing a steady course, the answer is yes. But God is not happy when men do things that involve their eternal loss. There is the story of Cain.[18] Cain did not bring an offering that indicated faith and trust in God or an acceptance of God's provision for his salvation.[19] God reasoned with him, but Cain went from bad to worse. Cain would not believe that God's dealings were just, and finally he "went out from the Lord's presence."[20]

Noah obeyed God and built an ark by faith.[21] For one hundred twenty years he preached to the antediluvians, warning them of a coming flood, but they would not believe and thus were destroyed. God was certainly in control of the elements, although He did not interfere with man's choice to do as he pleased and take the consequences.

Perhaps the outstanding story of God's dealing with His people is found in the Book of Exodus. In it we read about God's concern for the children of Israel while they were in Egypt and about His provision for their deliverance from bondage. It relates God's preparation of a leader in Moses, the struggle with the ruling powers in Egypt, the ten plagues, the crossing of the Red Sea, and the experience at Mount Sinai.

No Biblical narrative tells us more of God's control over the elements as He provided for a people who must travel through a desert land. But there is also His attempt to teach them His laws, the covenant He made with them, and the immeasurable patience He showed toward them. Could a people be more obdurate than the children of Israel in the wilderness? Yet God was gracious to them and fulfilled His promises by bringing them into the Promised Land.

Even in the land of Canaan the children of Israel did not always remain true to God or His commandments. Obviously a covenant based on man's promises to keep it was wholly ineffective in achieving its purpose.[22] Hence God in His mercy promised to make a new covenant. This new covenant would be effective because it would depend wholly upon the promises of God. He would write His laws on the people's hearts, and thus they would keep the law as a result of a new creation.[23] Furthermore, God sent His prophets to bring the children of Israel back to the allegiance from which they had wandered.[24]

Thus the children of Israel had a checkered career. They were taken into captivity and brought back. But God was in control. At times outstanding individuals like Daniel and his three companions gave a decisive testimony that God had His hand in the affairs of men.[25]

## God With Us

Matthew 21:33-41 relates a striking parable in which Jesus outlined God's dealings with His people. Jesus likened God to a landowner who planted a vineyard, provided all that was necessary for it to grow and produce, and handed it over to certain tenants. Then in accordance with usual practice he sent his servants to collect what was due him. But the tenants ill-treated every one of the servants, so the landowner decided to send his son. Surely they would respect his son! But no, the tenants treated the son in the same shameful way. Jesus then asked: "Therefore, when the owner of the vineyard comes, what will he do to those tenants?"[26]

The acme of God's love was manifested when He sent His Son.[27] He sent Him to be a humble babe in Bethlehem, to grow up subject to His parents, and when Jesus was baptized, God announced Jesus' identity by saying, "This is my Son, whom I love; with him I am well pleased."[28] But although Jesus came to what was His own, His own people did not accept Him.[29]

Can history be repeated in our day? Can we be callous to the presence of God in our midst? It is possible for us to act like the tenants of old, rejecting the One who has come for our salvation? The reading of history is a useless exercise unless we learn not to repeat the mistakes made by our forefathers.

Jesus said that He would build His church,[30] and with the church a new era is born. No longer are God's people limited to the members of one human family, the descendants of Abraham according to the flesh. God's people come from every kindred, tongue, and nation. Because they belong to Christ, they are the spiritual offspring of Abraham and inherit those promises God made to Abraham and his descendants.[31]

The church is, therefore, God's people today just as Israel composed God's special people in days of old. The church needs to be God-guided and God-controlled. It must be God's agency for accomplishing His purposes in the world. The challenge that comes to you and me is the challenge of faithfully fulfilling our God-given task. Shall we accept the challenge?

## Into All the World

God's mission in the world is not to condemn it but to save it.[32] It is only too easy to find fault. Members of the church must guard against this. No one was ever helped by criticism, except as the criticism was offered in love. This is not to condone the evil in the world but to point out that change and reform can take place only in an atmosphere of concern and understanding.

Jesus has commissioned the church to go into all the world and "make disciples of all nations."[33] This task is performed not by force but by persuasion. Not everyone will join the church and become a disciple. But a witness to the truth must be given, and everyone will decide whether to accept or reject it. It is when the gospel of the kingdom has been preached in the whole world as a "testimony to all nations," that the end will come.[34]

Your church today, then, is a special organization with a divine charter, a divine commission, and a divine task. It also has the Divine Presence as indicated by the vision John the revelator saw and then recorded in Revelation 1:12-20. Christ is in the midst of the churches to reprove,[35] exhort,[36] and encourage to greater zeal.[37] He offers to associate with the church if only the members will open their hearts to receive Him.[38] It is only your fault and mine if we do not seize our opportunities and make the church what it ought to be.

## Footnotes

1. Psalm 33:9
2. Hebrews 11:3
3. Hebrews 11:1
4. Hebrews 11:2
5. Genesis 1:10, 12, 21, 25, 31
6. Psalm 139:14
7. Isaiah 14:12
8. Ezekiel 28:12-15
9. Isaiah 14:14
10. Revelation 12:7-9
11. Genesis 3:13
12. 1 Timothy 2:14
13. Isaiah 46:10
14. Genesis 3:22
15. Habakkuk 1:13
16. Genesis 3:15
17. Romans 5:20
18. Genesis 4:1-16
19. Hebrews 11:4
20. Genesis 4:16
21. Hebrews 11:7
22. Exodus 24:1-8

23. Jeremiah 31:31-34
24. Hosea 6:5
25. Daniel 2:28; 3:17; 5:17-21
26. Matthew 21:40
27. John 3:16
28. Matthew 3:17
29. John 1:11
30. Matthew 16:18

31. Galatians 3:29
32. John 3:17
33. Matthew 28:19
34. Matthew 24:14
35. Revelation 2:4
36. Revelation 2:10
37. Revelation 3:11-13
38. Revelation 3:20

Chapter 2

# Firm Foundations

A structure is only as strong as the base upon which it is built. Jesus pointed this out when He contrasted the houses built on the rock and on the sand. The latter fell down with a crash when the winds and the rain beat upon it, but the former remained absolutely strong.[1]

An institution is only as strong as the support that it receives, and a kingdom will last only as long as its authority is recognized. An important factor in the rise of any nation is the righteousness of its cause and dealings.[2]

What about the church? What is its foundation? How strong and longlasting can we expect it to be?

Referring to his work as an evangelist, the apostle Paul asserted, "By the grace God has given me, I laid a foundation as an expert builder." He went on to say, "For no one can lay any foundation other than the one already laid, which is Jesus Christ."[3] In other words, as he went from place to place raising up churches, he did so by preaching about Jesus Christ. This was his only message. This was the basis of his success. In one instance he said, "May I never boast except in the cross of our Lord Jesus Christ."[4] For him, Christianity was Christ.

On this theme William Barclay, a great New Testament expositor, has said, "At best all our versions of Christianity are inadequate; but we would be saved much inadequacy if we tested them not by our own prejudices and presuppositions, nor by agreement with this or that theologian, but set them in the light of the New Testament and, above all, in the light of the Cross."[5]

But who is this Jesus that true Christianity affirms and evangelists proclaim?

## Inadequate Affirmations

19

Even in the time of Jesus the question of His identity was raised. Jesus Himself asked the question: "Who do people say the Son of Man is?"[6] Jesus frequently used the term *Son of Man* in referring to Himself. The disciples did not hesitate in their reply: "Some say John the Baptist; others say Elijah; and still others, Jeremiah or one of the prophets."[7] Apparently there were differing identifications given, and in this respect the world has not changed very much, because there are still varying descriptions given about Jesus.

If Jesus is central to the gospel, if He is the foundation of the church, then we must know who He is. We cannot be satisfied with hearsay. The Jews in the time of Jesus bypassed the issue when they said that He was John the Baptist. For one thing John and Jesus came from different mothers—Elizabeth and Mary. They were born about six months apart, so it could not be a matter of reincarnation, even if one could accept such a principle. Were the Jews suggesting that John's and Jesus' work was the same, a call to repentance? John had made clear that his work was a preparation for the Messiah, who would come after him.[8] The two could not be molded into one.

It is apparent that the Jews wanted to avoid the identification of Jesus with the Messiahship. This they did also when they identified Him with Elijah. Now Elijah was a well-known prophet from Old Testament times.[9] He had been caught up to heaven in a whirlwind. Could it be that he had come down from heaven? Once again a knowledge of the parentage of Jesus would rule this out. The Jews themselves had said on one occasion: "Isn't this the carpenter's son? Isn't his mother's name Mary, and aren't his brothers James, Joseph, Simon and Judas?"[10]

The same objection could be made to the identification of Jesus with Jeremiah. It is interesting to note that Jeremiah had announced the new covenant.[11] But Jesus is more than the *message* of the covenant. He is the *Maker* of the new covenant.

The last identification of Jesus as "one of the prophets" is a classic example of refusing to think any further. If He could not be identified with anyone they knew, then He must be identified with one they did not know. But once again it was a denial of what Jesus really was. They were giving Jesus high honor, because all the persons mentioned by name were highly regarded for their accomplishments. But it was not giving Jesus the highest honor.

When men and women today refer to Jesus as being a great teacher, they are telling the truth but not the whole truth. When they say that He was a prophet, they are denying what in Jesus is most essential, His deity. Nothing less is adequate. No less an affirmation is acceptable.

## A Basic Confession

After Jesus had asked His disciples what other people said about Him, He turned to them and asked: "Who do you say I am?"

The disciples were on the spot! He now called upon them to express their convictions. Had they really caught the message of Jesus? Did they really believe the message of the shepherds when they announced His birth?[12] Did they believe in the virgin birth? Had they seen in Jesus a personality that transcended the human?

It was the impetuous Peter who spoke up, the Peter who was never afraid to lead: "You are the Christ, the Son of the living God."[13]

Can you imagine the deathly silence that must have followed this solemn declaration of faith? Can you imagine the satisfaction that must have come to Jesus as He heard those words from the disciple of whom He had prophesied: "You will be called Cephas"?[14] The name in Aramaic means "rock," or "Peter" in the Greek.

One may well wonder why Jesus would call this disciple, at their first meeting, Rock. Did Jesus see in him certain characteristics that would justify such an appellation? The Jews customarily gave names to individuals that suited their nature, or names that parents hoped might be fulfilled in their children. James and John were called Boanerges, "Sons of thunder," because of their fiery temper, an example of which occurred when they saw how Jesus was treated by the Samaritans. They wanted to call fire down from heaven to destroy the inhospitable Samaritans.[15]

We may never know exactly why Jesus said that Simon Barjona would always be know by the name Peter. Of course Peter may well have been a "piece of the Rock" when he preached the pentecostal sermon. But he was not always the recognized leader in the early Christian community.[16] No doubt he considered himself, like all other followers of Jesus, a "living" stone coming to "the

living Stone,"[17] Jesus Himself, and being built into a spiritual
house.

God sees us not as we are in our sin but as we might be when
transformed by His grace. He is always optimistic about our
possibilities, and in this respect He is very different from the many
people around us.

The main thing is that Peter made a right confession. He
described Jesus as He really was. It is because Jesus is the Son of
the living God that He can save man and draw him up to God.

### Truth Revealed

Jesus' reply to Peter's confession indicated that Peter had not
arrived at his conclusion by human reasoning. He had not reached
this truth because a scholar had told him so. It was a truth that could
be grasped only by a revelation from heaven. "Blessed are you,
Simon son of Jonah," said Jesus, "for this was not revealed to you
by man, but by my Father in heaven."[18]

It is important to note than an understanding of who Jesus is
cannot be reached by logic or philosophy or the study of nature.
Here is something beyond the natural. Unless we recognize God as
the Creator and the Bible as His revelation, we cannot possibly
imagine how God could become man or how Jesus would be the
Son of the living God.

Jesus said that Peter was blessed in the knowledge he had
received and appropriated. Truth has a way of making man free.
Jesus had told His followers, "If you hold to my teaching, you are
really my disciples. Then you will know the truth, and the truth will
set you free."[19] A man is free when he knows the truth about God
and man and the world in which he lives. He is free because he
knows how to relate to every aspect of life. He is not a prisoner of
his doubts and questions. Blessed is such a man!

Science has made tremendous strides in recent years. Because
of advances in technology man can do amazing things. But so long
as science is limited to what can be tested in a laboratory, so long as
it has to do only with physical and material laws, it is limited in
scope. Man must understand that beyond the temporal values there
are those that are spiritual and eternal.

Man is indeed fortunate that God has condescended to reveal
Himself, to communicate with man and reveal His plans and

purposes. But man's mind must be open to recognize and accept God's revelation. It does not require education or a high standard of intellectual ability to grasp such a revelation. But it does require a willingness to be convinced by the evidence and to follow in the direction that the revelation leads. It means to be willing to accept the experience of the heart as well as the mind.

It is important, therefore, that the Christian diligently study the Word of God. And the Word of God is not far away from any one of us.[20] The church that has a program in which every member can study the Bible is indeed a strong church. And those members who avail themselves of the programs offered are the strong members. What kind of member are you?

## The Rock Foundation

After pointing out that Peter's understanding of Jesus' identity resulted from a divine revelation, Jesus made one of the most controversial statements in Scripture: ''And I tell you that you are Peter, and on this rock I will build my church.''[21]

Why did Jesus now refer to Simon as Peter, when before He had called him Simon son of Jonah? Was Jesus pointing to a connection between Peter as a name (because it means ''rock'') and the rock on which Jesus would build His church? If so, what is the connection? Did He mean that *Peter* and *rock* were synonymous terms and that Jesus would build His church on Peter, the rock?

The Roman Catholic Church has long averred that this is the case. But Protestants have argued that this cannot be the true interpretation. How can Jesus build a church on a human being, however good or perfect he may be? Peter doubtless had his good points, but he also had some outstanding weaknesses. For example, Paul had to oppose him openly in Antioch when he failed to practice the gospel and gave evidence of acting differently on different occasions.[22]

It is noteworthy that Peter never claimed to be the foundation of the church. In his letter to ''God's elect, strangers in the world, scattered throughout Pontus, Galatia, Cappadocia, Asia and Bithynia,''[23] he referred to Christ as the Living Stone, a Precious Cornerstone, the Stone the builders rejected but had become the Capstone.[24]

It is more reasonable to believe that Jesus is the Rock on which the church is built. A Christian writer has put the matter succinctly this way: "In the presence of God, and all the heavenly intelligences, in the presence of the unseen army of hell, Christ founded His church upon the living Rock. That Rock is Himself—His own body, for us broken and bruised."[25]

The psalmist asked an important question: "For who is God besides the Lord? And who is the Rock except our God?"[26]

What, then, is the connection between Peter and the Rock? Was Jesus using a mnemonic device to emphasize a point? Did Jesus look forward to the future and see that Peter would be "a piece of the Rock," in the sense that you and I can be living stones in the church? Certainly Peter had made an important confession, and anyone who can make such a confession is a "piece of the Rock." Peter on this occasion took the lead as he was to do on other occasions in his career. He may represent those who are solid members of the church, even though at times they may have their weaknesses. They are not the foundation of the church, but they are part of the building. Their understanding of Jesus and who He is and what He has done for them is as unshakable as a rock.

### Power to Survive

Jesus told Peter and the disciples that *He* would build *His* church. It is Christ who builds the church, not men or women. The church is not merely an association of men and women who meet together and form bonds of fellowship because they have common understandings and common aims. Common aims and common understandings they have, but they come together because Jesus has called them and Jesus has built them up. Jesus has brought them together.

Pastors and evangelists sometimes think that they build up the church, that they bring the saints out of the world. But all church leaders must recognize that they cannot do anything without Christ and that they are only humble instruments that God can and has used for the propagation of the gospel. It is God who has given the witness life. It is God who has given the seed of the word the power to grow.

Furthermore, the church is Christ's church. It owes allegiance only to Christ. The true church does not follow the lead of individuals or take its name from prominent leaders.

Because Jesus is the Founder, the Foundation, and the Builder of the church, the church is impregnable. To use the words of Jesus: "The gates of Hades will not overcome it."[27] The Greek word here transliterated "Hades" means the same as the Hebrew word *sheol*. It refers to the grave, the abode of the dead. Modern versions of the Bible bring this thought out clearly. Thus the New English Bible* translates it: "The powers of death shall never conquer it." The Revised Standard Verson renders it: "The powers of death shall not prevail against it."

Death is an enemy of man—an enemy of accomplishments and an enemy of continuity. But death will not adversely affect the church. Though men may die, the church will go on. Though death may seem to bring an end to man's accomplishments, the work of the church will never cease. The church rises above the individual because it represents the work of Jesus Christ.

Satan thought he had gained a victory when Jesus was placed in the tomb. But Jesus broke the bonds of that tomb by His resurrection, and ever since, the Christian can say, "Where, O death, is your victory? Where, O death, is your sting?"[28] Martyrs down through the centuries have mocked at death. They chose to be true to Christ and suffer death, because they knew that in Christ they had eternal life. The day would come when they would be raised to live with Christ forevermore.

Death is the wages of sin, but the gift of God is eternal life. Hence the church is indestructible, because it represents those who have accepted Christ and dwell in Him.

### Authority Confirmed

Jesus followed up His statement of the indestructibility of the church with a reference to the authority that the church would have: "I will give you the keys of the kingdom of heaven; whatever you bind on earth will be bound in heaven, and whatever you loose on earth will be loosed in heaven."[29]

What did Jesus mean by "the keys of the kingdom of heaven"?

Keys always imply authority and ready access. When you are

---

*From The New English Bible. Copyright, The Delegates of the Oxford University Press and The Syndics of the Cambridge University Press, 1961, 1970. Reprinted by permission.

given the keys of a car, you can use it any time you please. When you are old enough to receive the keys of the house, it means that now you can go in and out as you please. You do not have to ask for permission. You can lock the door to keep someone out or in. To receive the keys of a city is to receive a high honor.

In terms of the kingdom of heaven, the keys may well refer to the means of opening the doors of salvation so that men and women may walk in. Peter opened a door at Pentecost, and as a result of his work, thousands were converted in a day.[30] Peter opened a door in the home of Cornelius, and the firstfruits of the Gentiles came into the church.[31] Philip opened the door of salvation to the Samaritans, and Paul likewise opened doors of salvation wherever he went.

When people hear the words of the gospel and accept the provisions God has made for them, they receive forgiveness of sin, and they are loosed from the bondage of death. On the other hand, if they refuse the message of salvation, they remain bound in their sins.

Mrs. White has put the matter succinctly: " 'The keys of the kingdom of heaven' are the words of Christ. All the words of Holy Scripture are His, and are here included. These words have power to open and to shut heaven. They declare the conditions upon which men are received or rejected. Thus the work of those who preach God's word is a savor of life unto life or of death unto death. Theirs is a mission weighted with eternal results."[32]

The close connection between earth and heaven as brought out in the words of Jesus shows how closely heaven and the church are interrelated. No organization on earth can compare with the church in this respect.

Is Jesus suggesting that the church governs what happens in heaven? This can hardly be the case. J. B. Phillips in his translation of Matthew 16:19 puts it this way: "Whatever you forbid on earth will be what is forbidden in Heaven."[33] In other words, there is such close harmony between heaven and the church that the church never runs ahead of Christ. It knows what heaven stands for and teaches those things that harmonize with its principles.

## Footnotes

1. Matthew 7:24-27
2. Proverbs 14:34

3. 1 Corinthians 3:10, 11
4. Galatians 6:14

5. Barclay, William, *The Letters to the Corinthians* (Philadelphia: The Westminster Press, 1956), (paperback), p. 33.
6. Matthew 16:13
7. Matthew 16:14
8. Matthew 3:11
9. 1 Kings 17-19; 2 Kings 1, 2
10. Matthew 13:55
11. Jeremiah 31:31-33
12. Luke 2:11
13. Matthew 16:16
14. John 1:42
15. Luke 9:54
16. At the Council in Jerusalem James seems to have been the "president," although Peter significantly contributed to the discussion (Acts 15:1-21).
17. 1 Peter 2:4, 5
18. Matthew 16:17
19. John 8:31, 32
20. Deuteronomy 30:11-14; Psalm 85:9; 145:18
21. Matthew 16:18
22. Galatians 2:11-13
23. 1 Peter 1:1
24. 1 Peter 2:4-8
25. White, E. G., *The Desire of Ages* (Mountain View, California: Pacific Press Publishing Association, 1940), p. 413.
26. Psalm 18:31
27. Matthew 16:18
28. 1 Corinthians 15:55
29. Matthew 16:19
30. Acts 2:14, 41
31. Acts 10:44
32. White, *op. cit.,* pp. 413, 414
33. The New Testament in Modern English, Revised Edition. Copyright, J. B. Phillips, 1972. Used by permission of The Macmillan Company.

Chapter 3

# Community of the Called

One day Jesus said to the disciples, "You did not choose me, but I chose you."[1] This doubtless reminded them of how Jesus had called them one by one. Matthew had been sitting at the tax collector's booth when he heard the words: "Follow me."[2] Peter and Andrew were casting their nets into the Sea of Galilee when they were invited to be "fishers of men."[3] James and John were preparing nets in a boat with their father when Jesus called them.[4] Only one had proffered his services, and he was the one who betrayed his Lord.[5]

The Greek word for church, *ekklēsia,* has a form of the verb *kāleo* in it. *Kāleo* means "I call" or "I summon." Although etymology is not always a safe guide in deciding what a word means, it seems that the root meaning of the word *ekklēsia* is a "calling out." The word "was used among the Greeks of a body of citizens gathered to discuss the affairs of State, Acts 19:39. In the Sept. it is used to designate the gathering of Israel, summons for any definite purpose."[6] Thus the word referred to a recognizable body that met for a specific purpose and was summoned for this occasion.

In describing the early church Luke says that those who accepted the message of Peter's sermon at Pentecost "devoted themselves to the apostles' teaching and to the fellowship, to the breaking of bread and to prayer," and then he adds significantly, "And the Lord added to their number daily those who were being saved."[7] The divine initiative was seen in the growing size of the church, and a body was formed that had recognizable characteristics.

Although the church is primarily a New Testament phenomenon, it has its roots in the Old Testament, because the God who "added" to the church in the days of the apostles is the same God

28

who had called men and women to His service in days of old. Stephen in his speech before the Sanhedrin traced the dealings of God with the children of Israel and called them the "congregation in the desert."[8] God is always active in relation to men and women, and He continues to be active in the church today. Indeed, the church is the sphere of His continued activity throughout the world.

How and to what does God call? We shall seek to answer this question as we look at a number of Biblical examples.

## To Leave the World

According to Stephen, God's call to Abraham came in the words: "Leave your country and your people . . . and go to the land I will show you."[9]

There were good reasons why Abraham should leave his country and people. Although Ur enjoyed a high level of civilization, it was also a center of the worship of false gods. Nannar, the moon-god, was considered the owner of the city-state. He occupied a shrine on the top of a ziggurat sixty-eight feet high. Sir Leonard Woolley described the impressive structure and its influence as follows: "The Ziggurat, with its terraces planted with trees to give point to its name 'the Hill of Heaven,' dominated the entire city, and 15 or 20 miles away across the dead level of the plain the farmer looking up from his work in field or garden would see that towering shrine which was the actual dwelling place of the god his master. It was impossible not to be continually aware of the divine presence."[10]

In such an atmosphere of idolatry it would have been very difficult for Abraham to maintain his religious integrity as a monotheist. Abraham's father, Terah, had been infected by his environment and had served other gods.[11] The worship of the true God requires a separation from any situation that stands as a temptation. God asked Abraham to break family and national ties in order that he might become the father of the faithful.

We do not know how God communicated with Abraham, but we may be sure that Abraham had no doubts regarding the source of his communication. When one receives a call, it is always clear and undeniable. That is the only way God can be fair to man.

When Abraham obeyed the call, he had to exercise faith.[12] He was setting out to a destination not yet revealed to him. Could he really trust God to lead him every step of the way? Would God always provide for his needs? These questions often arise. But faith—absolute trust—never doubts God's promises.

Abraham was not perfect. He made mistakes. But God stayed with him and used him in His plans and purposes. In the experience of Abraham we see how God was active for good and the good that can be accomplished when man responds in trust.

## To Be God's People

As the Creator, God claims ownership of everything. The psalmist has expressed it this way: "The earth is the Lord's, and everything in it, the world, and all who live in it; for he founded it upon the seas and established it upon the waters."[13]

But not everyone recognizes God's ownership. Not everyone believes that He is the Creator.

Why? It is not easy to answer the question, but one of the basic reasons is that men and women refuse to accept the revelation that God has given in His Word. They will not accept the authority of the Bible. Thus they do not accept the account of Creation in the first two chapters of Genesis as authentic. If God is not the Creator of the universe, then it would be difficult to show that He owns or has a right to any of it.

Jesus told the woman of Samaria that God seeks those who will worship Him in spirit and truth, who will acknowledge Him for who He is.[14] When He finds them, He calls them to be His people.

God's people recognize the sovereignty of their Maker. They obey His laws because they find those laws right and good. They agree with the psalmist that "the Law of the Lord is perfect, reviving the soul."[15] They study the laws God has given so that their lives may be brought in harmony with them.

And in exchange for obedience God promises His people that He will own them and bless them.[16] Because He will protect them and prosper them, they will have an experience different from any other people.[17]

God designs that His people shall be witnesses to the world of the blessings that come as a result of allegiance to Him. In this way there will be an ever-living witness to God's goodness besides the witness of the Scriptures. Men and women will thus have the means of becoming acquainted with the God of the universe and of accepting Him and of being saved in His eternal kingdom.

The church is essentially God's people, owing allegiance to Him and reflecting His character. Do you recognize the privilege and blessing of being one of God's people, called to serve a holy purpose?

## To Forsake Darkness

Peter contrasted those who have accepted God and His revelation with those who have not accepted Him. He wrote: "Once you were not a people, but now you are the people of God." [18]

Can you imagine what it means to be without relations, to have no family members or no national connections? Some people have experienced this, and they have felt very lonely, almost helpless. Can you imagine what it is like to have no God to whom you can pray with confidence or to feel that you are adrift in a world without meaning? It is a frightening experience, a feeling of lostness.

Peter said that those who have entered the fellowship of God's people have now found new meaning to life. They know where they have come from and where they are going. They know that they have a God who sees and understands them. They know that whereas life was pretty rugged before, now it is full of grace and truth.

Peter used metaphorical language in referring to the difference between being out of the church and being in it. He said that one is the situation of being in darkness; and the other, of having entered into wonderful light. [19]

God has given you and me intelligence and the powers of reasoning. And He expects us to use these gifts. He does not expect us to live like brute animals and always remain in ignorance. The Christian has the privilege of searching for the truth and finding it. As a member of the church, he is not asked to accept any doctrine blindly. He is not to follow leaders blindly. He is expected to study for himself and to come to his own conclusions.

Jesus said, "I am the way and the truth and the life." [20] Only those who accept Him as their personal Saviour can know the blessedness of walking in light. They alone know the way that they ought to take. They know where truth can be found. And they also know that death is no threat because they have eternal life. As members of the church, they have been called from darkness into a wonderful light.

## To Be Disciples

A disciple is basically a learner. He listens to a teacher and does what the teacher asks him to do. The good teacher not only teaches with his words but also with his life. He sets an example that the disciple can follow. This is certainly true of Jesus.

Jesus has issued the following invitation: "Come to me, all you who are weary and burdened, and I will give you rest. Take my yoke upon you and learn from me, for I am gentle and humble in heart, and you will find rest for your souls. For my yoke is easy and my burden is light."[21] Church members are those who have heard His invitation and have accepted it.

Those outside the church find life wearisome and a burden. Why? Because a life led without a recognizable objective is boring, and a life lived without any external aid soon becomes burdensome. Furthermore, life is filled with obstacles to achievement, and lack of success leads to frustration. Selfish ambition never satisfies, and worldly pleasures soon lose their luster.

The situation is entirely different with the devoted church member. Having accepted the pattern of Jesus for his life, he finds he does things that bring joy and happiness to others as well as to himself. He does not feel burdened with guilt, because his sins have been forgiven. He is not concerned with what happens in this life, because he knows that he is assured of an entrance into the life to come. He finds that Jesus gives him the strength to meet the trials of every day, and he is encouraged by the victories Christ enables him to gain.

We read that Jesus "went around doing good."[22] Can you imagine a more satisfying occupation? The Christian in his church and in his community seeks to do all the good he can. He can find no greater happiness than that of following in the footsteps of his Master.

No task is too lowly if it is in the line of service. Jesus once washed His disciples' feet. Then He said, "Now that I, your Lord and Teacher, have washed your feet, you also should wash one another's feet. I have set you an example that you should do as I have done for you. . . . Now that you know these things, you will be blessed if you do them."[23]

Do you follow Jesus' example in the church service? Not many churches observe the ordinance of humility. Is there a reason for this? Some church members avoid taking part in this form of service. Do you think that they miss a blessing as a consequence?

## To Be of Service

The credit union to which I belong has the following motto: "Not for profit, not for charity, but for service." I think this is a beautiful motto. It suggests that at least one financial institution in the world does not have profit as its primary objective. "Not for charity" means that the institution makes a charge for necessary expenses but that it does not go beyond that. After all, legitimate expenses must be met in any cooperative venture.

Large corporations often advertise themselves as service organizations. They know that they can gain goodwill in this way. But are they always as solicitous of their customers' welfare as they claim? One gets the impression that their emphasis on service is a gimmick to protect their financial interests. Is not the world full of institutions that are concerned only to foster their own welfare?

In this regard the church must stand unique. God has called it to serve the needs of the world and not to bolster its own ego.

When Jesus called His disciples, He "gave them authority to drive out evil spirits and to cure every kind of disease and sickness."[24] In other words, He commissioned them to go out and meet some of the crying needs of the world. Mark reported that "they went out and preached that people should repent. They drove out many demons and anointed many sick people with oil and healed them."[25]

Is our church today spending its energies on serving the community, or is it more concerned about building up its own self-image? One gets the impression that some churches are more concerned about being large, prestigious, and influential. More money is spent on stained-glass windows, architecture, and facilities than on satisfying the needs of the poor. These churches want to ensure their right to exist, to engage in political programs, and to be much in the public eye. But as a fellowship they are cold and forbidding, open only to the rich and the well favored.

In a world full of tragedy and suffering, the church must remember that it exists to alleviate suffering and to point to the One

who heals all of our ills. Unless we do this, we fail in our call to
service.

## To Live Worthy of God

Paul wrote to the church of the Thessalonians: "You are
witnesses, and so is God, of how holy, righteous and blameless we
were among you who believed. For you know that we dealt with
each of you as a father deals with his own children, encouraging,
comforting and urging you to live lives worthy of God, who calls
you into his kingdom and glory."[26]

A life worthy of God! What kind of life is this? Paul indicated
what he meant when he related some of his activities in their midst.
He had dealt with them as a father, encouraging and comforting and
living a holy and blameless life. But to understand fully what he
meant we must remind ourselves of Paul's experiences in Thes-
salonica. The story is told in Acts 17:1-9. Paul preached convincingly about Jesus Christ and how He had fulfilled Old Testament
prophecies. As a result some of the Jews became Christians, as did
many "God-fearing Greeks and not a few prominent women."[27]
(This reference to women ought to convince men who are filled
with self-importance that women have an important role to fill in
the church!)

But jealous Jews rounded up "bad characters from the marketplace"[28] and started a riot. Paul had to remain in hiding, and under
cover of night he and his companion, Silas, were whisked off to the
road to Berea.

If you had such treatment, how would you feel? Would you
maintain proper decorum and still try to keep in touch? Or would
you feel bitter and disappointed?

To live a life worthy of God means to do your duty regardless of
the treatment you receive. Jesus lived that way, and you and I are to
live that way also.

Writing to the Ephesians, Paul elaborated on the life worthy of
the calling that has come to us as church members: "Be completely
humble and gentle; be patient, bearing with one another in love.
Make every effort to keep the unity of the Spirit through the bond of
peace."[29] Here is the ideal for every church member.

# Footnotes

1. John 15:16
2. Matthew 9:9
3. Matthew 4:18, 19
4. Matthew 4:21
5. There is an interesting account about Judas in Ellen G. White's book *The Desire of Ages,* pp. 716-722. "He felt a desire to be changed in character and life, and he hoped to experience this through connecting himself with Jesus. . . . But Judas did not come to the point of surrendering himself fully to Christ" (p. 717). Here was the secret of his failure.
6. Vine, W. E., *An Expository Dictionary of New Testament Words* (Old Tappan, NJ: Fleming H. Revell Company, 1966), Vol. I, p. 84.
7. Acts 2:42, 47
8. Acts 7:38
9. Acts 7:3
10. Woolley, Sir Leonard, *The Beginnings of Civilization* (New York: Mentor Books, 1963), p. 119.
11. Joshua 24:2
12. Hebrews 11:8
13. Psalm 24:1, 2
14. John 4:23
15. Psalm 19:7
16. Exodus 19:5
17. Deuteronomy 7:12-15
18. 1 Peter 2:10
19. 1 Peter 2:9
20. John 14:6
21. Matthew 11:28-30
22. Acts 10:38
23. John 13:14-17
24. Matthew 10:1
25. Mark 6:12, 13
26. 1 Thessalonians 2:10-12
27. Acts 17:4
28. Acts 17:5
29. Ephesians 4:2, 3

# Chapter 4

# Distinguishing Characteristics

If I look for the church, can I find it? What are its distinguishing characteristics? These practical questions demand answers.

At the outset, we need to remind ourselves that the church as presented in the New Testament is composed of disciples. Men and women formed a corporate entity to which letters were written and messages given. In this sense the church is visible, and anyone who seeks for it should find it.

Whether everyone who claims to be in the church really belongs in it is another matter. In this sense the church may not be wholly visible. Furthermore, the church has existed for many centuries, and many of its members have long since passed away. In this sense the church is obviously not wholly visible. Yet the church may be the subject of historical study. Its growth and development may be known as far as records and documents are available.

Since the church has a visible presence, we can reasonably ask about its characteristics. In this way we can identify the church. We can also distinguish between the true and the false, assuming that counterfeit churches may exist.

In the first place we need to distinguish between external and internal characteristics of the church, between the material and spiritual aspects of its life and existence. Whereas there may be a correlation between what a church looks like and what it is, what it is is more important than its surface appearance.

Sometimes a church may be confused with its building. Some people cannot conceive of a church apart from a building with a steeple or a cross on it. But the church is more than the building. It is the people who use that building.

Sometimes a church is confused with a denominational organization. Now a church needs to be organized and in most instances needs to have a name and a legal status. But the church is more than its organization or leadership. In some cases the church could exist without being a legal entity, and its organizational structure may be very simple.

The life of the church will lead to buildings and to the setting up of leadership and organization, but these are externals. They will vary from place to place and from time to time. They will reflect differing cultures and languages and traditions. But these external features will always remain true to the spiritual and internal life of the church. It is this aspect of the church that we need to study.

Notice that the church is both one and many. There is only one church, and it owes allegiance to one Lord. Yet this one church exists in many locations. Each church is a whole—*the* church—whether it is at Rome or Constantinople, yet it is mystically part of the one church throughout the world. Is this concept difficult to grasp? Perhaps so, but then the church as a whole is difficult to comprehend. We stand before a mystery, and we must accept by faith what Scripture reveals.

What, then, according to the Bible are the distinguishing characteristics of the church? We shall consider six of them.

## Confessing Jesus

Luke described the early church immediately after Pentecost: "Day after day, in the temple courts and from house to house, they never stopped teaching and proclaiming the good news that Jesus is the Christ."[1] That is, the early disciples told everyone they met that it was their conviction that Jesus of Nazareth had fulfilled the Messianic prophecies of the Old Testament.

Before the Crucifixion the disciples had believed that Jesus was the Messiah. But the Crucifixion had come as a shock. Their hopes that Jesus would redeem Israel were dashed to the ground. Then came the Resurrection, and Jesus spoke with two disciples on the road to Emmaus: "How foolish you are, and how slow of heart to believe all that the prophets have spoken! Did not the Christ have to suffer these things and then enter his glory?"[2] He then went on to show how the life and experience of Jesus were revealed in the Old Testament.

Having witnessed their risen Lord, the disciples were ready to see the Old Testament prophecies in a new light. And after receiving the outpouring of the Holy Spirit, they had a message that they could deliver with unprecedented power. When told to desist from preaching Jesus because their message was embarrassing the leaders of the Jews, they said that they had to obey God rather than man: "For we cannot help speaking about what we have seen and heard."[3] In fact, they prayed: "Now, Lord, consider their threats and enable your servants to speak your word with great boldness."[4]

In Antioch the disciples were first called Christians.[5] That is, they were emphasizing the Messiahship of Jesus—the lordship and the salvation that He brings. Most commentators have suggested that the name was given in scorn as a nickname. But a prominent Christian writer has said: "It was God who gave to them the name of Christian. This is a royal name, given to all who join themselves to Christ."[6]

The church is, therefore, a group of people whose prime emphasis in life and teaching focuses on Jesus Christ and what He means to them. Nothing will prevent them from giving their testimony. They are not only Christian in name but in heart.

## Loyal to Truth

Jesus said to His disciples, "Simply let your 'Yes' be 'Yes,' and your 'No,' 'No'; anything beyond this comes from the evil one."[7]

Man so habitually prevaricates that on important occasions he will be asked to take an oath that he will tell the truth, the whole truth, and nothing but the truth. The Christian does not mind taking such an oath when it is necessary to do so. But the fact is that he speaks the truth at all times, and he speaks it in love.[8] He will have nothing to do with falsehood, because he knows that all lying is of the devil. Jesus said of the devil: "When he lies, he speaks his native language, for he is a liar and the father of lies."[9]

Truth sometimes hurts, but if the hurt is to heal, then it is good. At times, however, it is best not to speak the truth. For example, it is best not to speak evil of anyone, even though the assertion may be true. Such statements are judgmental, and none of us is in a position to judge.[10]

The member of the church remains loyal to the truth, not only in the sense that he speaks the truth with his neighbor but also in the sense that for him Jesus is the truth.[11] All that Jesus stood for revealed truth. All that He revealed of God the Father was true.

Jesus was the very embodiment of truth.

This means that the Christian considers truth to have an objective reality. Truth exists apart from himself and independently of him. Truth is not relative to the viewer. Man either does or does not perceive truth. But the man who sees Jesus looks at the truth of God and man and the relations that exist between the two. The Christian is, therefore, positive in his understanding of truth, and he feels he can be loyal to it.

The Christian also feels that he can find the truth in the Bible as the Word of God. He feels he must be loyal to its precepts. In fact, he feels that the Bible is part of that truth which has a sanctifying influence,[12] and he joins all those who study and seek to understand it.

By contrast, those who are not willing to accept God's revelation of Himself only end up serving the creature rather than the Creator. As a result they embroil themselves in all kinds of filthiness and unseemly behavior.[13]

## Doers of the Word

The story is told of a parishioner who went to his priest and asked to be taught passages of Scripture. The priest was surprised but delighted. He quoted the command: " 'Love your neighbor as yourself.' Go home, learn the commandment, and come back tomorrow for another passage of Scripture," the priest instructed.

The parishioner went home, but he did not return the next day. A week passed, and the priest met him on the street. "Say, friend," the priest asked, "how is it you have not come back for more Scripture to learn? Haven't you learned the verse I gave you?"

"Oh, yes," replied the parishioner, "I've learned to say the words, but I've not been able to put them into practice."

The parishioner had the right idea. It is no use reciting Scripture without putting its precepts into practice. Jesus pointed out the same truth when He said that in the judgment some people would claim to have used His name but without obeying what that name stands for, that is only pretense and hypocrisy.[14] Christians are "doers of the word."[15]

Too many Christians are Christians in name only. The Muslim world looks upon the Western world as Christian. But they hear of crime and violence, murder and rape, divorce and the use of drugs, and the portrayal of all kinds of evil in films and on television. They say: "If that is Christianity, we shall have none of it." And who can blame them? The missionary to the Muslim must point out that true Christianity has nothing to do with evil. It sets a high standard of conduct for every individual. Members of the true church do not engage in the practices of the world.

A Christian is not a Christian because he has been born into a Christian family. Neither is he a Christian because he lives a fairly clean life or knows the doctrines of the church. Nicodemus thought he was a candidate for the kingdom of heaven because he was a ruler of the Jews and as far as the law was concerned he was perfect. But Jesus told him that he had to be born from above.[16] In other words, only the born-again Christian can be a doer of the word because only the power of God enables anyone to keep the spirit as opposed to the letter of the law.

### Reacting in Love

The man who takes pride in his piety can be an obnoxious prig. His attitude is not at all attractive. But the one who is motivated by love in all that he does draws others to himself.

Jesus said to His disciples: "All men will know that you are my disciples if you love one another."[17] Love among the members serves as a distinguishing characteristic of the church.

In commenting on Jesus' command to His disciples to love one another, William Barclay emphasizes that they were to love as Jesus loved. He goes on to point out that Jesus' love had four important characteristics:

1. Jesus loved selflessly. His love was outgoing, whether the love was returned or not. As human beings, too often we love only those who love us, but such a love centers in the self and is not the ideal love that we should have in the heart.

2. The love of Jesus was sacrificial. It did not cringe at the possibility of the cross. Love always makes us vulnerable, but love will not count the cost of loving.

3. Jesus loved His disciples understandingly. He knew their weaknesses and failings, but He loved them just the same. He loved Judas even when He knew that he would betray Him. He longed to save him. True love is not blind in the sense that it ignores the characteristics of its object. It may love the black sheep even

more than the ninety-nine who are safe in the fold, because the black sheep needs more love.

4. Jesus loved forgivingly. Peter denied Him three times, but He did not hold it against him. True love is always ready to forgive and to forget. It holds no grudges and asks for no compensation.[18]

Have you found a church with members who show such love for one another? Do you yourself show such love? The world hungers for love and understanding, and it is only by the grace of God that the church can offer to the world what it needs.

## Seeking Revival

Your church today must never feel that it has "arrived." Like the apostle Paul it must recognize there is always room for improvement. There is always *plus ultra*—more beyond.

Paul expressed his need to press forward in the following words: "Brothers, I do not consider myself yet to have taken hold of it. But one thing I do: Forgetting what is behind and straining toward what is ahead, I press on toward the goal to win the prize for which God has called me heavenward in Christ Jesus."[19]

Note the steps in this attitude:

1. The Christian does not consider himself to be perfect. He is not self-satisfied. He is not confident that he knows the truth, that he is "in the truth," and that there is nothing more for him to learn. Some Christians leave the impression that they always know what is right and do it. Have you ever met such a person? If you have, do you really think he is right?

2. The Christian forgets the records he has achieved in the past—the money he has contributed to the church, the number of people he has baptized, or the responsible positions he has held in the community as a church leader. These things may give him a sense of pride. They will boost his human ego and make him pharisaical.

He also forgets his failures—the times when he sowed his wild oats and the wasted years when he could have done much more than he did. These things can so discourage him that he forgets the value of his own soul to God. He feels that it is useless to try to do any better and that in the future he will repeat the failures of the past. It is not profitable to live in the past and to let the past govern the present. However, when we remember the way God has led and provided for all our needs, the past can give us the basis of confidence in the future.

3. The Christian presses forward toward the highest goal of all—perfection in Christ. Paul put it this way: "I press on to take hold of that for which Christ Jesus took hold of me."[20] In other words, he wanted to fulfill the purpose for which he was created and to accomplish the task for which he had been called.

Churches, and sometimes individuals, have a way of holding on to tradition. They cannot accept new ways of doing things. They forget that sometimes the old ways of looking at things may get in the way of Bible truth. Jesus pointed out this danger to the Jews because some of their traditions nullified the Word of God.[21] It is important, therefore, to compare what we do with the principles of the Bible to make sure that we have not been led astray. This is not to shake the foundations but to make sure that we stand on solid ground in every position we take. And let us not be afraid of making changes if changes are necessary.

*Revival* and *reformation* are key words in the experience of the true church. Is your church vibrant and alive, or is it stultified, barren, and cold? Take the temperature of your church by comparing it with the picture given in Revelation 2:4, 14, 16, 20 and 3:2, 16.

### Doing God's Work

The church must always be sure that it is doing God's will, reflecting His image.

The danger exists that the church will spend more of its time fostering its own interests than in meeting the needs of the community. It may be more interested in statistical growth than in witnessing to Jesus Christ. It may spend more money on buildings and facilities than on preaching the gospel. When this is the case, it becomes an institution, but it fails to be the channel of God's activity.

When Jesus commissioned His disciples to go into all the world, He intended that they should continue the work He had begun. For this purpose He endued them with power. And as long as the church has been doing this, it has been powerful. But when the church wants to be rich and increased in goods; when it wants political clout in order to effect social changes, however good these changes may be; when it wants to pass laws favorable to its ideas and thus to compel compliance, then we must write over the church doors: "*Ichabod*, . . . the glory has departed."

God wants the church to be the depository of His grace, the agent of reconciliation. Therefore, it is primarily concerned with changes in the heart and mind. When it feeds the body, it wants to feed the soul as well, for the feeding of the body is temporal, but the feeding of the soul has eternal consequences.

In doing God's work the church may not always be popular, but the church is not in a popularity contest. Jesus warned His disciples that their work would not always be received with favor. And He cautioned them not to be elated by words of praise.[22] As long as the church remains in the world and as long as it does what God wants it to do, it will face opposition in the world—just as Jesus Himself was rejected by the majority.

Is our church today enjoying divine favor, or is it failing in its mission?

## Footnotes

1. Acts 5:42
2. Luke 24:25, 26. Some of the texts that Jesus may have used would be: Isaiah 7:14—the virgin birth and the name Immanuel, which means "God with us"; Micah 5:2—the birthplace, Bethlehem; Zechariah 13:6—betrayed by His own disciple and rejected by His own people; Psalm 22:18—garments distributed by lot. But more especially Isaiah 53, where we read: "He was pierced for our transgressions, he was crushed for our iniquities" (verse 5). Jesus is the Lamb that takes away the sins of the world.
3. Acts 4:20
4. Acts 4:29
5. Acts 11:26
6. White, E. G., *The Acts of the Apostles* (Mountain View, California: Pacific Press Publishing Association, 1911), p. 157.
7. Matthew 5:37
8. Ephesians 4:15
9. John 8:44
10. James 4:11, 12
11. John 14:6
12. Compare the prayer of Jesus, John 17:17
13. Romans 1:18-32
14. Matthew 7:21-23
15. James 1:22, KJV
16. John 3:3
17. John 13:35
18. The above outline has been taken from William Barclay, *The Gospel of John:* Vol. 2, pp. 173-175, but the author has added some of his own interpretations.
19. Philippians 3:13, 14
20. Philippians 3:12
21. Mark 7:13
22. Luke 6:26

Chapter 5

# Meaningful Metaphors

Since the church represents God's activity among those who respond to Him in obedience, we must understand the life of the church in terms of relationships. What is the relationship between God and His people?

The question is not easy to answer, because God is infinite and man is finite. God is perfect in character and understanding, while man is very imperfect and very limited in his grasp of the infinite. How can these two diverse entities communicate and maintain a living and growing relationship? The problem is not with God but with man.

Because of the uniqueness of the phenomenon it is difficult to find parallel relationships between man and man or between man and the material universe. In fact, it is impossible, given the nature of Christ and the church.

Paul, writing to the church in Ephesus, referred to the close relationship between husband and wife, how the two become one, and he added, "This is a profound mystery—but I am talking about Christ and the church."[1]

We must not be misled by the modern meaning of the word *mystery*. Vine explains it thus: "In the N.T. it denotes, not the mysterious (as with the Eng. word), but that which, being outside the range of unassisted natural apprehension, can be made known only by Divine revelation, and is made known in a manner and at a time appointed by God, and to those only who are illumined by His Spirit."[2]

Thus the relationship between Christ and the church is not something secret. Rather, it can be understood only by one who is willing to recognize what is revealed and to accept that revelation. Only the one "inside" the church can really know what the relationship means.

44

The Bible uses a number of metaphors to describe the relationship between God and His people. No metaphor is complete in itself, but every metaphor adds a special meaning of its own that, when added to the insights of the other metaphors, significantly contributes to the meaning of the whole. Only as we look at the whole can we begin to fathom the depths of the mystery that is the relationship between Christ and the church.

In this chapter we shall look at six metaphors used by Bible writers.

## Sheep and Shepherd

In our modern, industrialized world it is becoming rare to find people who have seen sheep, let alone those who know anything about the relations between the shepherd and his sheep. In our era of mass production and of doing everything on a large scale, even sheep farms have lost much of the personal touch that once characterized the caring for sheep. But when Jesus said, "I am the good shepherd," He was saying something immediately recognizable and appreciated by His hearers. The image was not only clear, but it was also full of an emotional quality that made it vivid.

If you want to know how real the imagery of sheep and shepherd could be to people in the Middle East, we need only to remind ourselves that Adam's second son, Abel, kept sheep.[3] Moses spent the second forty years of his life caring for sheep in Midian.[4] As a boy King David shepherded a flock and proved his prowess so that he was qualified to fight Israel's Philistine enemy, Goliath.[5]

If we want to know how good a shepherd can be and what he does for the sheep, we can read Psalm 23. The psalmist said that he was fortunate to have the Lord for his Shepherd because he would not lack anything that was for his good. He knew what it was to have his food abundantly supplied, and he found his life cast in pleasant places. His spiritual needs were supplied, and he found himself doing those things that were right in everyone's eyes. When called upon to go through difficult times he received companionship and comfort. At the same time he enjoyed honor and respect before his enemies, and he expected to experience love and fellowship in the house of the Lord forever. Can any relationship be more beautiful than this?

Sheep are very much like people. They are dependent on leaders for guidance and protection. Sometimes they get lost and need to be found. When they are young, they need to be carried. They often go astray, and they need patience and understanding in handling. Jesus added the thought that the good shepherd will give his life for the sheep.[6] Thus we see that the church member has nothing to fear but everything to gain from his relationship as a sheep to a shepherd.

## Branches and Vine

If the metaphor of sheep and shepherd suggests a closeness between one and the other, the imagery of branch and vine suggests an even closer tie.

The vine referred to here is the grape vine, a plant that produces a delicious fruit, and from the fruit comes a wholesome drink. When the spies came back from the land of Canaan, their evidence that the land flowed with milk and honey included a single cluster of grapes so large that two men had to carry it on a pole.[7]

Branches, then, can be very valuable for bearing precious fruit, but they can do so only by remaining on the stem of the vine. From the stem they receive the vital sap that keeps them alive and enables them to bear fruit. Any of the glory of fruit bearing does not come from the branch but from the vine.

This connection between the branch and the vine stem is so important that if the branch is connected with a wild stem, it will produce wild grapes. It is not only the connection that is important but also the connection with the right stem. And if the branch is not vitally connected with the stem, then it is not good for anything. It is not good for construction purposes. It is not good for making furniture. It can only be thrown away and burned.

Furthermore, the vine needs pruning from time to time so that it can produce well. Useless branches need to be cut off so that they do not draw strength from the vine and prevent it from achieving maximum benefit. Jesus said: "My Father is the gardener."[8] Just as a gardener watches over his plants and provides them with everything they need, so God has made provision for His people. And they have no one to blame but themselves if they fail to accomplish what God designs to do in and through them.

Thus we see from the metaphor of the vine and the branches that the church cannot do anything good except as the members maintain a vital connection with their Lord. Furthermore, the good that they do does not redound to their personal glory but to the glory of God.

Isaiah 5:1-7 points out how God has made every provision for His people. The figure of speech is that of a vineyard set on a fertile hill. The ground is well prepared. The choicest vines are planted. Provision is made for protection and the processing of the grapes into wine. But the vineyard does not respond as expected. What a tragedy when the church does not do what the Lord expects of it because members have failed! Are you and I responding as we ought? Do we maintain a close connection with God every day so that He directs our every step?

### Stones and Building

We think of a building as something more permanent than vines or branches, or sheep and shepherds. It must be this thought of permanency that is brought out in the metaphor of stones placed in a building. The church is not a transitory organization. It is a permanent structure.

Yet it seems incongruous to liken people to stones. Perhaps because of this Peter referred to "living stones."[9] He was guilty of perpetrating what is called a mixed metaphor. But here we have an example of the difficulty in drawing parallels of the church from human situations. Everyday examples will never exactly illustrate church relationships. This fact should not stop us from seeking suitable illustrations, but it does caution us from expecting to understand fully what the church is like from any one situation.

Let us consider further this imagery of stones and building. What can it tell us about the church? Here are some suggestions, apart from the one already made.

1. A stone by itself is not very valuable. It needs to be bonded with other stones. No Christian should think that he can do anything alone. He must be associated with others in the fellowship of the church.

2. A stone will need hewing and shaping if it is to find a suitable place in the building. We are not by nature good. God needs to remake us if we are to find a place in His structure.

3. All stones, even when they are bonded together, are depen-

dent on the cornerstone if they are to form part of a finished building. The church ceases to exist if it does not make Jesus Christ the very center of all its activity. Closely related to this concept is that Jesus must be the foundation of every doctrine. All truth, all preaching, must be related to Him.

The apostle Paul also used the metaphor of a building in describing the church. He said, "You are God's field, God's building."[10] He referred to himself as a builder, but he built for God. He had carefully chosen a solid foundation on which to build—Jesus Christ.[11] Writing to the Ephesians he elaborated on this concept: "Consequently, you are no longer foreigners and aliens, but fellow citizens with God's people and members of God's household, built on the foundation of the apostles and prophets, with Christ Jesus himself as the chief cornerstone. In him the whole building is joined together and rises to become a holy temple in the Lord. And in him you too are being built together to become a dwelling in which God lives by his spirit."[12] The church is a holy temple, and every member is a temple in which the Holy Spirit dwells.

## Kingdom and King

We live in a day when there are very few kings. And of the kings that exist few are absolute monarchs. There may be very good reasons for this. The fact that the Bible talks about a king and a kingdom does not mean that we should attempt to set up political monarchies. But the concepts of a king who rules effectively and authoritatively and of the kingdom over which he exercises benevolent rule can help us understand what Jesus meant when He talked about the church He would build.

Jesus' first message was: "The time has come. . . . The kingdom of God is near. Repent and believe the good news!"[13] His message that the kingdom over which God would rule was near was good news to be accepted and believed.

For centuries kingdoms had risen and fallen. Daniel had forseen these in the dream God had given to Nebuchadnezzar.[14] But Daniel had also seen that the time would come when the God of heaven would set up a kingdom that would never be destroyed. This kingdom is more important than any other kingdom. And we must prepare for it.

What did Jesus mean by the "kingdom of God" or the "kingdom of heaven"? Matthew 13 records a number of parables that explain the expression. It is "like a man who sowed good seed in his field. But while everyone was sleeping, his enemy came and sowed weeds among the wheat, and went away."[15] It is action. It is God at work. There is enemy action too. But the time of harvest will come. The good will be gathered in, and the bad will be thrown away. Note God's singular concern that none of the wheat be damaged by inconsiderate action.

The kingdom of heaven is like mustard seed—small to begin with, but its growth is phenomenal compared to its beginnings. It is like yeast working silently but effectively to leaven the whole lump. It is like hidden treasure or a pearl of great value that is worth all the sacrifice expended for it. It is like a net that gathers in good and bad. In other words, the kingdom of heaven is the highest good for which anyone may strive.

Jesus admitted to Pilate that He was a king.[16] He even had servants who would fight for Him. But His kingdom was not of this world. It is a spiritual kingdom, concerned with spiritual values. His subjects fight, but they fight the good fight of faith.[17] For attack and defense they use the whole armor of God.[18] Their citizenship is not primarily on earth, but in heaven.[19]

## The Household of God

If the concept of a kingdom and a king makes the relationship of the church member to his Lord too distant, then the concept of the household of God comes in as a salutary correction. Paul combined these two concepts in one verse, thus letting one complement the other.[20]

What is there new in the imagery of a household? It is the relationship based on family connections. There is one Father and many children, who are brothers and sisters.

As soon as we talk about a family we refer to a common parentage. Ties of blood always bring us closer together. Blood is thicker than water, we say, and we mean that the loyalties between child and parent and brother and sister are difficult to break. These loyalties transcend all others. But it also means that there will be family likenesses, inherited characteristics that will distinguish a member of the family from one who is not.

It is important to note that church members resemble each other, not because they have adopted the same principles or have taken up the same kind of discipline, but because they belong to the same family. At one time they belonged to the family of the first Adam. But then they became members of the family of the second Adam.[21]

As Christians we are fairly conversant with the concept of the second birth. But to Nicodemus the thought of being born again came as a shock. He thought he was good enough. After all, he was a ruler of the Jews and had lived an upright life. But Jesus said he would never see the kingdom of heaven if he were not born again.[22]

The trouble with us Christians is that we may be very pharisaical at times. We may legalistically suppose that we can earn our way into heaven. We may think that because we have been baptized and because our names are written in the church books we are guaranteed a place in heaven. But we must die daily and rise daily to walk in newness of life.[23] Only thus can we be true members of the church.

As members of the household of God we have a family name.[24] But more importantly we inherit the characteristics of our heavenly Father. We behave like Him because we are His children and partake of His nature.[25] That is why Jesus said to His disciples: "Be perfect, therefore, as your heavenly Father is perfect."[26]

## Head and Body

Perhaps the most striking Biblical illustration of the relation of Christ to the church is that which speaks of Christ as the head and of the church as the body. Here we have not only the intimacy of connection but also the absoluteness of direction.

The interdependence of head and body is remarkable. Not only is the body useless without the head, but the head is useless without the body. The church is God's agency for reaching out into the world, and thus the church is a very important organ to Him. We must never belittle the importance of the church in God's overall plans and purposes.

Now the body has many members, and each has a separate function from the others. But they all cooperate under the direction of the head. There is thus a unity in the apparent diversity. No member should claim that he is more important than another, for every member is needed to supplement the work of the others. If there is any priority in the church, it is only in the headship of Jesus Christ.

Sometimes the body is diseased, and the various members cannot coordinate as they should. Those of us who have seen people suffer this way cannot help but feel sorry for them. By contrast, the muscle and movement of an athlete are beautiful to watch. Everyone would like to achieve the goal of perfect coordination within himself, because it gives a feeling of well-being. So it is with the church. Only as the various parts coordinate smoothly can it be an object of admiration and respect. The more diverse the parts and the more perfect the coordination, the greater the glory.

Jesus gave His authority and power[27] to His disciples so they could take the gospel into all the world. Why did He do this? Because from that time on Jesus would be in the world through His disciples.[28] They would do His work and represent Him. They would even be treated as He was treated.[29] When the world sees the church, it should see Jesus Christ in all its activities, because Jesus Christ lives in the heart and life of every member.

Does this sound too idealistic for you? It is the truth, if we accept the testimony of God's Word. If we fall below the ideal set before us, we should humbly ask for forgiveness, renew our vows of devotion to Christ, and seek to maintain a living connection with our Lord. Then our prayer shall be: "Direct, control, suggest this day/All I design, or do, or say,/That all my powers, with all their might,/In Thy sole glory may unite."[30]

## Footnotes

1. Ephesians 5:32
2. Vine, W. E., *An Expository Dictionary of New Testament Words,* Vol. III, p. 97.
3. Genesis 4:2
4. Exodus 3:1
5. 1 Samuel 16:11; 17:32-37
6. John 10:11
7. Numbers 13:23
8. John 15:1
9. 1 Peter 2:5
10. 1 Corinthians 3:9
11. 1 Corinthians 3:10, 11
12. Ephesians 2:19-22
13. Mark 1:15
14. Daniel 2
15. Matthew 13:24, 25
16. Mark 15:2
17. 1 Timothy 6:12
18. Ephesians 6:11
19. Philippians 3:20. The KJV has "conversation." The true meaning is "citizenship."
20. Ephesians 2:19
21. 1 Corinthians 15:45-49
22. John 3:1-8

23. Romans 6:2-4
24. Ephesians 3:14, 15
25. 2 Peter 1:4. Peter adds that by participating in the divine nature we "escape the corruption in the world."
26. Matthew 5:48
27. Matthew 16:19; 10:1; John 20:21-23
28. Matthew 10:40
29. Matthew 10:24, 25
30. Thomas Ken, in *The Church Hymnal* (Washington, D.C.: Review and Herald, 1941), No. 44, third stanza.

Chapter 6

# The Way of Holiness

Jesus pointed out that a person can choose one of two ways in this life.[1] One way is narrow. The other is broad. One has a narrow gate through which to pass. The other has a broad one. Most people take the broad way, but some, a few, take the narrow road. The narrow road leads to eternal life, but the broad way leads to eternal destruction.

Why do so many take the broad way? Jesus does not give us the answer. Perhaps the majority of people prefer an easy life, one in which they do not have to expend much energy or exercise much discipline. Apparently they feel unconcerned about the end of the road. They spend their time thinking of the present.

However, a few are concerned about the end of the road, and they want life. They know that the narrow road will involve hardship now, but they feel that the goal of life is worth it. They know that restrictions now will mean freedom later. They recognize that anything worth having is worth working for. So they willingly forgo a certain amount of pleasure now for the greater pleasure later. They have made a choice based on foresight.

Life on this earth is largely a matter of making decisions. We choose what we want to do and what we want to be. There are limitations to our choices, of course, limitations of locality and environment, talents and skills, and opportunities that come our way. But basically we decide whether we want to take the easy road of pleasure or whether we shall discipline ourselves in order to reach well-defined goals. Our choice determines our destiny.

Those in the church have decided to take the narrow road that leads to eternal life. They have chosen to accept certain forms of behavior as normal, and they have adopted certain goals as natural. Peter expressed one of the goals in these words: "Just as he who called you is holy, so be holy in all you do."[2]

Holiness! That is a high standard indeed. Can a man who is a sinner by nature be holy? What do we mean by *holy?*

One principle needs clarifying: A man cannot make himself holy. Paul brought this thought out when he pointed to Christ as the One who makes people holy. "Once you were alienated from God and were enemies in your minds because of your evil behavior. But now he has reconciled you by Christ's physical body through death to present you holy in his sight, without blemish and free from accusation." Then he went on to say: "This is the gospel that you heard and that has been proclaimed to every creature under heaven, and of which I, Paul, have become a servant."[3]

The member of the church is to tread the way of holiness. There is no other way. The writer to the Hebrews added the solemn thought: "Without holiness no one will see the Lord."[4] It is important, therefore, to find out what the way of holiness implies.

### Called to Be Saints

In current English a saint is generally one who has been canonized by the church. He has lived an exceptionally holy life and, having died, is considered to be in heaven where he can intercede for sinners.[5] But the Biblical usage of the word *saint* differs. Therefore, a number of modern translations of the Bible use other terms than saint when this word occurs in the KJV. Here are some of the expressions used for Romans 1:7:

"Called to be his dedicated people" (New English Bible).

"Called to be his own people" (Today's English Version*).

"Called to be Christ's men and women" (The New Testament in Modern English, by J. B. Phillips).

However, the Jerusalem Bible, the New American Standard Bible, and the New International Version retain the word *saint,* presumably because it can be understood in the light of New Testament usage.

What is the New Testament usage? In the plural form it refers to Christian believers in general. It does not single them out as persons of exceptional holiness.[6] Thus Ananias referred to the members of the church at Jerusalem as saints.[7] And Peter accord-

---

*From The Bible in Today's English Version. Copyright, American Bible Society, 1976.

ing to Luke visited the saints at Lydda.[8]

At the same time we must not lose sight of the fact that the English word *saint* comes from the Latin word *sanctus,* which means "holy." Paul wrote to the church members at Rome that they were "called to belong to Jesus Christ" and "called to be saints."[9] He also urged them, "in view of God's mercy, to offer . . . [their] bodies as living sacrifices, holy and pleasing to God—which is . . . spiritual worship."[10]

Thus the saint is not merely a believer, one of God's dedicated people belonging to a particular community. He also recognizes God's goodness and mercy to him, and in response he offers his talents and life to Him in daily service, to be used as God sees best. The word *sacrifice* reminds him that anciently sacrifices were to be without blemish.[11] Therefore he renounces his old life of sin and commits himself to obeying God's commands. Worship for him is more than a ritual of adoration performed at certain times in particular places. It is his whole life of dedicated service.

If the church member is truly this, he is a special person indeed. But we Christians need to be reminded constantly that God has called us to this kind of dedication.

## Meaning of Holiness

The Bible reveals that holiness in the absolute sense is distinctively and primarily an attribute of God alone. The psalmist said that the Lord is holy and His name is holy.[12] Scholars say that God is holy "in the sense that He stands utterly above the created world; He is the wholly other, the incomprehensible, the unanalysable, the unfathomable."[13]

That which is separated for God's service is called holy. Thus the ark, the temple, the furnishings in the temple, and the altar were all sacred objects.[14] Jesus pointed out that the altar could make the gift offered on it sacred.[15] However, in the last resort the source of all holiness is God. For example, God set apart the seventh day of the week and made it holy. Thus He commanded men to remember it and to *keep* it holy.[16]

Because God is holy, His presence renders the ground holy when He is present. Moses at the burning bush had to remove his sandals as a sign of reverence for God because the ground he stood on was holy.[17] Joshua had a similar experience.[18] God's presence on Mt. Sinai was a frightening sight to behold, and the people had to make adequate preparations before they could approach the foot of the mountain.[19]

A holy God cannot look on evil or tolerate wrong.[20] For this reason man in God's presence gains a wholesome recognition of his sinfulness and unworthiness. Isaiah felt overwhelmed when in the temple he "saw the Lord seated on a throne, high and exalted."[21] But then he received cleansing, an indication that God does not want to overawe or to destroy but to cleanse and purify.

The proper response to God's holiness is to honor Him[22] and to keep His commandments. This concept of fear sounds strange to Christians, who believe that God is love, but even the New Testament tells us to fear God[23] and to give Him glory.[24] This fear springs from a recognition of the danger of displeasing God. It arises out of our love for Him. Have you noticed that a lover always fears hurting the beloved?

We belittle God when we fail to approach Him with respect and reverence. The poet has put the matter succinctly: "Before Jehovah's awful throne, Ye nations, bow with sacred joy; Know that the Lord is God alone; He can create, and He destroy."[25]

## The Divine Imperative

God is holy, and He also wants His people to be holy. He wants them to reflect His character of love and benevolence and of righteousness and peace. Holiness in a very real sense connotes wholeness.[26]

But it is God who makes holy, and when He makes His people holy, the nations will recognize this holiness with respect and fear. God has always wanted His people to occupy a position of honor in the land,[27] but this depends on their keeping His commandments and following His instructions. Then God can add His many blessings, so that they prosper in all that they do. They will be the "head, not the tail" and always "at the top, never at the bottom."[28]

Paul made it clear that holiness involves avoiding all sexual immorality.[29] God's people are to be different from the godless people around them. It is tragic when church members fall into the same sins as those outside the church! When it comes to marriage and divorce, the mores of the community should not decide standards, but God's revelation and God's Word.

In His intercessory prayer Jesus prayed that God would sanctify His disciples, or make them holy.[30] He indicated that this would be done "by the truth" and that God's "word is truth." In other words, God's revelation of truth would direct the disciples in the way of holiness. That is why the Christian accepts the Bible as the Guidebook in matters of principle and life-style.

When Peter wrote to God's chosen people,[31] he reminded them of the divine imperative: "Be holy, because I am holy."[32] It is a privilege and an honor to be chosen by God, but it also involves a responsibility. God expects them to live a life of obedience and holiness. William Barclay has put it very well: "The Christian is God's man by God's choice. He is chosen for a task in the world, and for a destiny in eternity. He is chosen to live for God in time, and with God in eternity. In the world he must obey the law of God, and reproduce the life of God. The Christian has been chosen by God, and, therefore, in his life there must be something of the purity of God and in his action there must be something of the love of God. There is laid on the Christian the task of being different."[33]

## The Believer's Response

Although God sanctifies the believer, the believer is not a passive recipient. God has given him the capability of intelligently deciding and the power to act. Just as God is a person, so man, created in God's image, is also a person. God does not force Himself upon anyone, neither does He compel action. But the Christian responds to God's love, and so John could write: "Everyone who has this hope in him purifies himself, just as he is pure."[34]

John, in extolling God's love, said: "How great is the love the Father has lavished on us, that we should be called children of God! And that is what we are!"[35] In other words, God has revealed His love by calling us His children. And we are not children merely in name. We are children in fact, for God has already made us His children. Consequently we are to become like Him. This will occur most completely at the Second Advent. But the Christian is doing something about it even now. He keeps his life "from being polluted by the world."[36]

The Book of Hebrews is very specific: "Make every effort to live in peace with all men and to be holy; without holiness no one will see the Lord."[37] The greatest blessing that can come to anyone is to see the Lord. The Christian has found that the secret of his success has been in fixing his eyes upon Jesus.[38] But his sight has been of the mind and the understanding. At the Second Advent he will see Jesus face-to-face. He will stand among those who will look up and say: "Surely this is our God; we trusted in him, and he saved us. This is the Lord, we trusted in him; let us rejoice and be glad in his salvation."[39] He will not be among those who cover their faces and call upon the rocks to hide them from "the face of him who sits on the throne and from the wrath of the Lamb!"[40] But in order to qualify for this experience he must take time to be holy while he lives here on earth.

This means that he must steer clear of all those sins that the wicked are guilty of committing. Paul listed some of them in his first letter to the Corinthians.[41] Because the Christian has been washed, sanctified, and justified "in the name of the Lord Jesus Christ and by the Spirit of our God,"[42] how can he go back to a life of disobedience and shame?

Thus the church member must live a life entirely different from that pursued in the world. He is separated and holy.

## Practical Aspects

Positive interrelationships exist between one member and another in the church. Paul referred to a number of these in Romans 16. Let us see what they imply.

1. The exchange of greetings. When one greets another, he indicates friendship. Nowadays many of us greet one another with a warm handshake. In some parts of the world a hug accompanies the handshake. Peter closed one of his letters with the exhortation: "Greet one another with a kiss of love."[43] Paul told the Corinthians: "Greet one another with a holy kiss."[44] Is there a suggestion here that some kissing may not be appropriate?

The form of a greeting may vary from place to place. Some greetings may only be a showpiece. Jesus criticized some who craved greetings in the marketplace because they liked to hear the titles of honor conferred upon them.[45] This kind of greeting does not belong in church circles. And some greetings waste too much time. They hinder one from completing a task in a reasonable amount of time.[46] But God can bless the greeting that wishes peace upon a person or a house. It will bring happiness in its train.

Do you feel ignored sometimes? Do people pass you by without acknowledging you? Unfortunately we all fail to do our duty at times, but happy is the church where members greet one another with warmth and good wishes.

2. Kindness and hospitality. There are always members who move from place to place. What a blessing when the church they visit receives and welcomes them into its fellowship! Some may have letters of introduction and may have served their home churches in a creditable way. They are certainly worthy of honor and should be treated accordingly. Paul listed a deaconess, fellow workers, hard workers, relatives, and friends. Some may be mothers and sisters. Regardless of sex, all should be treated equally with kindness and respect. If they need any help, financially or in business, we should offer such help. Even total strangers should be entertained cordially, because some "have entertained angels without knowing it"[47]

Do some of our churches lack the spirit of hospitality? Is kindness seldom shown to those in need? Why do you think this is? Can it be that God's love burns but dimly in the hearts of many members? It is not for us to judge, but surely we can look at ourselves and improve our ways.

## Blameless Lives

Paul set some high standards for the Christian. All of them relate to the way of holiness that is the only way a Christian can go. It is good to remind ourselves of these standards. Only in this way can we see how far short we may be falling from the ideal and what we should do to get back on the straight course.

Writing to the Philippians, Paul said, "Do everything without complaining or arguing."[48] Have you seen a home that does not have this problem of arguing and complaining? It is very human to object about a heavy task assigned to us. "Why cannot someone else do it?" we ask. And then the argument begins!

It takes much grace not to grumble and complain. Dare I say it? It takes a holy person to tackle every task as a duty and a responsibility and not to object to inequities and injustices. But this is the standard set before the Christian.

To a large extent we adopt the practices of the people around us. Someone finds fault with a situation and voices his complaint. Others take up the refrain. Thus it was with the children of Israel in the wilderness. Usually the solution to their problem was simple because God was always there with the answer. But how much easier it would have been if they had not grumbled or found fault or complained!

If church members were to walk in the way of holiness, they would be "blameless and pure, children of God without fault in a crooked and depraved generation."[49] Notice each word and its implications.

*Blameless:* William Barclay comments as follows: "The word which is translated *blameless* is *amemptos,* and expresses *what the Christian is to the world.* His life is of such purity that none can find anything in it to blame, or with which to find fault. It is often said in courts of law that justice must not only *be* just, but must *be seen* to be just. The Christian must not only be pure, but the purity of his life must be seen by all."[50]

*Pure:* This expresses *what the Christian is in himself.* It suggests absolute sincerity of thought and motive and character.

*Without fault:* This expression describes *what the Christian is in the sight of God.* The Christian can stand fearlessly under the scrutiny of God Himself.

Here, then, is the acme of perfection, walking in the way of holiness. Can any standard be higher? Thank God we can achieve it through Jesus Christ our Lord.[51]

## Footnotes

1. Matthew 7:13, 14
2. 1 Peter 1:15
3. Colossians 1:21-23
4. Hebrews 12:14
5. Compare for example *Webster's New World Dictionary*
6. Vine, W. E., *An Expository Dictionary of New Testament Words,* Vol. 3, p. 315.
7. Acts 9:13
8. Acts 9:32
9. Romans 1:6, 7
10. Romans 12:1
11. Malachi 1:8-13
12. Psalm 99:9; 111:9
13. P. Bonnard, in *A Companion to the Bible,* ed. J. J. Von Allmen (New York: Oxford University Press, 1958), p. 166.
14. Exodus 29:37; 2 Chronicles 35:3; 1 Kings 8:4, 6
15. Matthew 23:19

16. Genesis 2:3; Exodus 20:8-11
17. Exodus 3:5
18. Joshua 5:15
19. Exodus 19:10-23
20. Habakkuk 1:12, 13
21. Isaiah 6:1
22. Numbers 20:12, 13; 27:14
23. Isaiah 8:13; 29:23
24. Revelation 14:7
25. Isaac Watts, in *The Church Hymnal,* No. 1, first stanza.
26. Deuteronomy 28:10-14
27. Isaiah 58:13, 14
28. Deuteronomy 28:13
29. 1 Thessalonians 4:3-8
30. John 17:17
31. 1 Peter 1:1
32. 1 Peter 1:16
33. Barclay, Wm., *The Letters of James and Peter* (Philadelphia: The Westminster Press, 1960), p. 222.
34. 1 John 3:3
35. 1 John 3:1
36. James 1:27
37. Hebrews 12:14
38. Hebrews 12:2
39. Isaiah 25:9
40. Revelation 6:16
41. 1 Corinthians 6:9, 10
42. 1 Corinthians 6:11
43. 1 Peter 5:14
44. 1 Corinthians 16:20
45. Matthew 23:5-7
46. Luke 10:4
47. Hebrews 13:2
48. Philippians 2:14
49. Philippians 2:15
50. Barclay, Wm., *The Letters to the Philippians, Colossians, and Thessalonians,* p. 54.
51. Philippians 4:13; Romans 7:24, 25

Chapter 7

# The Shadow of Sin

After reading the last chapter, which pictured the church as walking in the way of holiness, one may ask: Where is that church? Does such a church exist?

In all humility Christians have to admit that they fall far short of the ideal set before them. And yet we may ask: Does the church cease to exist when its members fail?

Paul faced a similar question when he thought of the history of his own people, the Jews. On the one hand, they had been entrusted with the very words of God. Yet on the other hand, they had failed to live up to the light they had received. "What if some did not have faith?" he asked. "Will their lack of faith nullify God's faithfulness? Not at all! Let God be true, and every man a liar. As it is written: 'So that you may be proved right in your words and prevail in your judging.' "[1]

In other words, God's activity does not need man's validation for its success. God is independent of anything that man may do. Although the whole world may reject the mercy of God, that mercy remains fixed and established.

An important part of the mystery of the church is that it embodies an apparently insoluble paradox. The church is holy, and yet every member in it is a sinner!

That is why the church is such a difficult phenomenon to describe or to understand. Two sides to the church intermesh. One is the divine, and the other is human. In terms of God's activity, the church is holy and just and good. In terms of human response it is too often weak and failing.

We can express the paradox in a different way. When we see how few men respond to God's love, we may think that God has failed. He has failed to win all men to Himself. Yet when we look at those frail human beings who have dedicated their lives to serve mankind (and some of them suffered at the stake for what they knew to be the truth), we exclaim, "What saints!"

The shadow of sin then covers the way of holiness. In order to understand the church we must study the relation between holiness and sin within the Christian's life.

## The Presence of Sin

We all recognize the presence of sin in the world. What surprises most of us is that sin exists in the church. How can we reconcile sin with sainthood?

We begin by looking at some verses in the Bible that tell us about sin in the church. John insisted, in simple and clear language: "If we claim to be without sin, we deceive ourselves and the truth is not in us."[2]

What kind of man claims he has no sin? Perhaps he is the one who does not blame himself for the sin that he has committed, but instead he pins the blame on his heredity or environment. He says, for instance, "If my parents had not had such bad tempers, I could have been much sweeter in nature." Or, "If only I had grown up in a different environment I would not be the drug addict I am today." Some have blamed other individuals for leading them astray. Some will "borrow" other people's property, or cheat, and say that they are not stealing. Still others will claim that it is not wrong for *them* to do something, although it may be wrong for *others!* Have you ever heard of a double standard?

It is human to blame others for our wrongdoing, to seek to minimize or excuse the fault. Our first parents were guilty of this from the very beginning. But the fact is that sin is sin. Seldom, if ever, can we escape responsibility for what we have done.

Because we have been born into the family of Adam, we have inherited tendencies to sin. Jesus referred to this when He said to Nicodemus, "Flesh gives birth to flesh."[3] It is "natural" to sin, and as Paul so forcefully stated, "All have sinned and fall short of the glory of God."[4] Thus it does not matter whether we are Jew or Gentile, educated or simple, self-controlled or licentious. We all fall into the same category of sinners.

In one area we all have to admit that we have failed, and that is in the use of the tongue. Have we ever kindled a fire with a little word that we have let slip? James referred to the tongue as a small part of the body, but it can do and has done considerable damage.[5]

The difference between the sinner in the world and the sinner in the church is that the former has done nothing about his sin, but the latter has confessed it. Perhaps that is why saints seem to be such big sinners. They admit that they have done wrong! However, there is another difference. Unconfessed sin remains the responsibility of the wrongdoer, but confessed sin can be and is forgiven. And the wrongdoer is purified from all unrighteousness.[6]

## Our Filthy Rags

Most of us try to do something about our faults. We try to correct them and improve ourselves. Some of us do a fairly respectable job. You doubtless have met people who are upright in character and eager to do what is good, kind, generous, hospitable, humble, and gracious. The community holds them in high regard. If they are not already members of the church, we would be proud to have them join.

But the Bible will not let us take any credit for ourselves. Isaiah under inspiration wrote: ''All of us have become like one who is unclean, and all our righteous acts are like filthy rags.''[7]

When Adam and Eve sinned, they became conscious of their nakedness. Immediately they set about to do something for themselves, and they picked fig leaves for coverings. You can well imagine the inadequacy of this covering. Then, according to Scripture, God made garments from skins for them.[8]

The fig leaves and the skins represent a contrast. One represents what man plucked and made for himself. The other represents what God provided for them. The one would wither and die in a short time. The other would last through changing seasons and would provide warmth and protection as well as covering.

Man has always tried to work out his own salvation. He wants to atone for his own sin. But in this regard he is helpless. Having sinned, he comes under the condemnation of the law, and he can find no escape.

Some try to win God's favor by keeping His law. Some, even in the church, meticulously pay their tithe and keep the Sabbath. But often they ''have neglected the more important matters of the law—justice, mercy and faithfulness.''[9] They have zeal, but no love. And as Paul has so well said, anything that a man may do, however talented or sacrificial, if it is not accompanied by love, it is worthless,[10] like filthy rags.

Man can be saved only if God provides salvation, and here is where faith comes in. In order for our worship to be acceptable, it must be mingled with faith. Cain soon found this out.[11] We must accept the provision that God has made for our salvation and express this faith in modes relevant to it. In Old Testament times this meant a blood sacrifice that looked forward to Christ. And in our own times it means accepting Jesus as our personal Saviour.

The poet has put it beautifully: "There was no other good enough/To pay the price of sin;/He only could unlock the gate/Of heaven, and let us in. O dearly, dearly has He loved!/And we must love Him too,/And trust in His redeeming blood,/And try His works to do."[12]

### Saints Who Failed

When we recognize our faults and failings, we know that we are in no position to judge others. Yet it encourages us sometimes to know that others have made the same mistakes.

The Bible has frankly recorded the lives of the men of old. Great men, mighty leaders, God's own people, have not always lived free from sin. Abraham, the father of the faithful, revealed a basic weakness when he fearfully concealed the true identity of his wife, Sarah.[13]

Moses showed great faith when he "refused to be known as the son of Pharaoh's daughter" and chose to be associated with his despised and mistreated people.[14] Yet he proved his own human weakness when he lost his temper and smote the rock instead of speaking to it as God told him to.[15] As a result God did not allow him to enter the land of Canaan.

God especially chose David to serve as king of Israel. David won a signal victory over Goliath as he went "in the name of the Lord Almighty."[16] Yet he was guilty of a double sin when he sought to marry the already married Bathsheba and then arranged for the death of her husband.[17] The inspired recorder of the incident made this simple comment: "But the thing David had done displeased the Lord."[18] Is it any wonder? Nevertheless it was possible for Samuel to refer to David as a man after God's own heart![19]

In the New Testament we have the account of Peter's denying

his Lord three times. Yet God used him with great power at
Pentecost.

What does all this mean? How do we interpret the fact that
outstanding men of God have made bad mistakes, nay, have even
been guilty of undoubtable sin? John makes the situation perfectly
clear when he said: "He who does what is sinful is of the devil,
because the devil has been sinning from the beginning." But then
he went on to distinguish between committing a sin once and
sinning as a regular practice. "No one who is born of God will
continue to sin, because God's seed remains in him; he cannot go
on sinning, because he has been born of God."[20]

Here, then, we gain a true understanding of the relation of sin to
the saint. A saint is a sinner who renounces his sin. He confesses it
and has it forgiven. The sinner who lives a life of unremitting sin
can never be a saint.

### Need for Reform

John the revelator was directed to write to seven churches, and
in so doing he has summarized the history of the Christian church
from the first century to the end of time. His summary is well worth
study if we wish to know important truths about the church. For one
thing, we shall note that the church constantly needs reform.[21]

The first thing to note is that the churches have specific names.
The church has an address. The church can be seen. It consists of
people who are alive and real. The church is not some invisible
entity that cannot be reached.

The next thing to note is that the church serves as a center of
light to its community. God represents it as a number of golden
lampstands.

The third thing to note is that a glorious being walks in the midst
of it, obviously Jesus Christ. He holds the seven angels, or mes-
sengers, or leaders, in His right hand. He may do this for protection
or direction or both.

As soon as we read the messages to the churches, we find that
the churches have both strong points and faults. Thus the first
church has forsaken its first love. God warns that if it does not
return to its first love, it will lose its place as a lampstand. Love to
God and man must be the prime characteristic of the church.
Without loving concern, loving action, it ceases to exist as a

church.

The second church does not have anything recorded against it, so it may be that some churches are very close to the ideal. But the third church harbors those who hold and teach false doctrine. The church cannot remain true to its nature and condone evil at the same time.

The fourth and fifth churches have serious faults. One not only tolerates sexual immorality but apparently encourages it by lack of decisive action. The other is asleep and inactive even though it has a reputation for being alive.

God commends the sixth church for its constancy and tells it to expect the Second Advent soon. But the seventh and last church is lukewarm and self-deceived.

The picture drawn is that most churches need to mend their ways. In some respects they are fulfilling their obligations, but many need to repent and improve their relationship with Christ, or they will be lost in oblivion.

What about our church today? Is there anything we ought to do about its spiritual condition?

## The Tragedy of Sinning

The church has an entity of its own, but it can hardly be distinguished from its members. When we see the members, we also see the church. That is why every member should so live that he represents the church aright.

When any member sins, a blight covers the whole church. Paul expressed the possibility of this happening in the words: "God's name is blasphemed among the Gentiles because of you."[22] Paul was talking about his people, the Jews. They were a privileged community. God had chosen them, communicated His law to them, and established a covenant relationship with them. He had given them a knowledge of His will and had illuminated the past as well as having revealed His plans for the future. Indeed, they had received so much light that they could consider themselves teachers to the rest of the world. But Paul's searching questions probed into their unsavory past. They had not lived up to their privileges. On the contrary, they had been breakers of the law. As a consequence they had been taken into exile, there to be under the control of the despised Gentile.

Paul's logic in this instance is unanswerable. Obviously a people who have privileges should live up to them. And the church should too. But does it?

Does the member of the church, who knows the gospel, rejoice in it? Is he bearing an effective witness of God's goodness to him? Or is he leading a life of misery and uncertainty? Does he have a form of godliness that is obviously put on, because the laxity of his principles and life indicate that his religion has no power to change him for the better?[23] If so, then the nonmember seeing his example has no incentive to join the church. In fact, the church member may dishonor God by opening the door to strong accusations against the church.

Just as the children of Israel brought shame to their God when they worshiped other gods that were really no gods,[24] so members of the church will dishonor their own God and Lord when they fail to be separate and distinct from the world, when they follow worldly fashions, and when they mold their activities according to the practices of the world rather than the teachings of the Bible.

Do you find such a condition in our church today?

## A Prayer for Mercy

I think we can see the church struggling heavily under the shadow of sin. What shall we do about it? I fear that it is easy to find fault. The critics of the church are legion. Some find fault with prophetic interpretation. Others find fault with the leadership. Some want to change policies, while others do not want to make any changes at all. Have you noticed that the critic always points his finger at someone else?

It is unrealistic to think that the church has no faults. But it is also clear that a purely critical spirit never reformed the church. Rather than point at people, we need to point to the truth, not to find fault with practice, but to indicate a better way of doing things. We need to approach the church's problems positively. We should seek solutions rather than palliatives and seek to build up rather than to tear down.

Perhaps the best spirit we can show is to recognize that, for the most part, we are responsible for the problems that exist. We need to go to God and ask for mercy. We need to say with the psalmist: "Have mercy on me, O God, according to your unfailing love;

according to your great compassion blot out my transgressions."[25]

In this regard, the great prophet of Babylon, Daniel, has set us an example.[26] We would do well to read his prayer as recorded in Daniel 9. Although Daniel could well think of himself as upright and dedicated to his God, he nevertheless included himself when he confessed the sins of his people. "We have sinned and done wrong," he said. "We have been wicked and have rebelled; we have turned away from your commands and laws."[27]

The trouble with most of us in the church is that we are too self-righteous. We take pride in not being guilty of the wrong that we see about us. As a result we do not do anything to make the church what it ought to be. We do not seem to realize that when the church goes down, we go down with it.

At the same time, we must not suppose that we are the ones to bring about change. We can plant a seed and water the ground. But it is God who gives the increase. We need to pray that God will make *us* what we ought to be, and then the *church* will be what *it* ought to be.

## Footnotes

1. Romans 3:3, 4
2. 1 John 1:8
3. John 3:6
4. Romans 3:23
5. James 3:1-12
6. 1 John 1:9
7. Isaiah 64:6
8. Genesis 3:21
9. Matthew 23:23
10. 1 Corinthians 13
11. See the story in Genesis 4:3-5 and compare it with Hebrews 11:4.
12. Cecil Frances Alexander, in *The Church Hymnal*, No. 126, stanzas 4, 5.
13. Genesis 12:11-13
14. Hebrews 11:24-26
15. Numbers 20:8-12
16. 1 Samuel 17:45
17. 2 Samuel 11:2-27
18. 2 Samuel 11:27
19. 1 Samuel 13:14
20. 1 John 3:8, 9
21. This section will concentrate on Revelation 1:9-20 and chapters 2 and 3. These passages of Scripture should be read as a background to the present discussion.
22. Romans 2:24. Read from verse 21 to get the full impact of the statement.
23. See 2 Timothy 3:5
24. Ezekiel 20:27
25. Psalm 51:1
26. Daniel 9:4-19
27. Daniel 9:5

Chapter 8

# Unity in Christ

Many Christians talk about unity, but few know what they are really talking about. Most people will admit that unity in the church is desirable, but not many can tell you how to achieve this goal. Is it organizational and administrative unity that is needed? or is it unity of doctrine and teaching? or is it some kind of spiritual unity?

No one will deny that the Protestant world has fractured into many disparate units. But how can the various parts be brought together? At the same time, there are two other important segments in the Christian world: the Roman Catholic Church and the Eastern Orthodox community. Can the Christian world be united?

The divisions in Christianity cause embarrassment in the mission fields. For instance, ask a Muslim to become a Christian, and he will want to know, "Which branch of the church shall I join?" Furthermore, rivalry exists between the various Christian groups as to territory and power. Often the accusation and counteraccusation of "sheep stealing" arise when one member of a group changes his membership to another.

It is understandable, therefore, that a strong move toward uniting all the churches would occur. For over seventy years now the ecumenical movement has been growing. But it has had problems; problems of not having universal support, problems of doctrine and ritual. What can constitute the basis of unity?

Interestingly enough, there are two ways of approaching the problem of unity. On the one hand, the Protestants would like to unite their various elements and then make it possible for the Roman Catholic Church to join. On the other hand, the Roman Catholic Church feels that it is the mother church and that the "separated brethren" should return to her fold. Do you see a solution to the problem?

Perhaps at the outset we should consider the difference between being different and being divided. Churches can vary in size, in language used, in style of worship, in types of architecture for their buildings. But they need not be divided. They become divided only when one church accuses the other of heresy and claims to be the true church.

All groups that work for unity in the church use the Bible as their source and inspiration. But one thing is certain, the Bible emphasizes a spiritual unity, a unity of relationship with the Lord of the church, rather than a structural unity. Let us study what the Bible says about unity.

## One and Only One

Writing to the Ephesians, Paul said that there is "one Lord, one faith, one baptism; one God and Father of all, who is over all and through all and in all."[1] Clearly then, God is the Author and Source of all unity. To seek unity without understanding God and His activity is to seek a unity on a human level that may work satisfactorily for social organizations, but it cannot be satisfactory for the church. The church represents primarily God's activity, and it is only in God and from Him that true unity can exist. An external unity without a unity of relationship is valueless.

Paul pointed out that the unity of the church consists in allegiance to one Lord, the Lord Jesus Christ. He alone is the object of adoration, and He alone is the One to be obeyed. This will involve a recognition of who He is, according to the Scriptures, and a determination to follow His teaching and example.

There is one faith, that is, a believing experience in the one Lord by which one can be saved. As Peter put it: "Salvation is found in no one else, for there is no other name under heaven given to men by which we must be saved."[2] Such salvation comes by faith because it is God who purifies the heart by faith,[3] and He makes no distinction between Jew or Gentile. Paul said that he lived "by faith in the Son of God."[4] It is this faith, this trust in God, this acceptance of God's plans and purposes, that characterize the Christian, but it is a relation that is not visible to the eyes. Therefore a member may or may not be a true member of the church regardless of his denominational affiliation. Any form of unity that neglects this relationship is spurious.

There is one baptism, said Paul. This is a baptism "into Christ

Jesus,'' which is a baptism ''into his death'' and a rising to ''live a new life.''[5] It is a baptism by immersion, because only this method properly symbolizes burial and rising. This one ceremony indicates entrance into the church because it reveals a break with the past and the acceptance of new principles of conduct.

Notice, too, that one is not baptized into a church or a denomination. Baptism is into Christ in the name of the Father and the Son and the Holy Spirit. One is accepted into the fellowship of the church subject to baptism, or after baptism, and is extended the right hand of fellowship by representative leaders in the church. One may transfer membership from one church to another, but baptism is normally a one-time experience indicating allegiance to the one Lord by faith.

Thus there is only one church, determined not by race or nationality but by God's infinite grace and man's ready response.

## One in Christ

All those who work for the unification of the church quote Jesus' prayer in John 17 for doing so. Since the prayer reveals as much about the Lord of the church as it does the kind of unity that should prevail in the church, it will be profitable to study Jesus' prayer carefully.

Some have called it a high priestly prayer, because in it Jesus offers His life as the Lamb of God that ''takes away the sin of the world.''[6] His life was not taken away from Him, but He laid it down Himself.[7] He was thus both the sacrifice and the sacrificing priest.

As Jesus contemplated the death He would die, it was not easy for Him.[8] But for this purpose He had come into the world. Hence He prayed for Himself as He came to the closing scenes of His earthly ministry. ''Father, the time has come. Glorify your Son, that your Son may glorify you'' (John 17:1). He asked that His experience on the cross might fully and finally display God's love. He also desired that the experience might bring Him the glory He had ''before the world began'' (verse 5).

The closeness between the Father and the Son is evident. On the one hand, the Father had sent the Son (verse 18). The Father had ''granted him authority over all people'' (verse 2). On the other hand, the Son would glorify the Father (verse 1). The Son had completed the work God had given Him to do (verse 4). Thus the Father and the Son are inseparable in all that is done for the salvation of men.

It is in this context that we learn of the relationship between God and Christ and the members of the church. The disciples of Jesus were given to Him by the Father "out of the world" (verse 6). "They were yours," said Jesus; "you gave them to me and they have obeyed your word" (verse 6). Jesus took no credit for them, not even any credit for the message that He gave them. "Now they know," prayed Jesus, "that everything you have given me comes from you" (verse 7). As for the disciples, they had accepted the revelation given to them. They had been obedient. And for them this would be eternal life, to know the true God for what He is and Jesus Christ whom He had sent for their propitiation and reconciliation (verses 17-19).

When Jesus prayed for His disciples, He asked the Father, "Protect them by the power of your name—the name you gave me—so that they may be one as we are one" (verse 11). He said He gave them the glory that had been given to Him so that they would be one as He and the Father were one: "I in them and you in me" (verses 22, 23). These words stagger the imagination. Can any unity be more complete?

Obviously such a relationship is personal. It makes the church a unique phenomenon without parallel in any earthly organization. Therefore, to talk about unifying the church by means of human structures is unthinkable. The church is one because God makes it so.

## The Secret of Unity

Man in his fallen nature creates barriers and causes divisions. Human pride makes one think more highly of himself than he ought to think. Thus our respect for one another differs with one's wealth or education or family connections. We form cliques and give some people to understand that they are not wanted or welcomed. Can such a situation exist in the church?

Unfortunately too often we hear of a prejudice in the church that excludes people of certain races. Pride of occupation or position causes some to snub others. But we need to ask forgiveness for these sinful attitudes. How can people who cannot get along on earth ever hope to get along in heaven?

The secret of unity in the church is in having the same attitude to life that Jesus had.[9] Although He was God, He did not consider it beneath His dignity to become a man in order to save man. In fact, He accepted a very humble position as a man. He went so far as to endure the cruelest of indignities. For this reason God has raised Him to the highest of positions, and everyone will bow in acknowledgment of His power and authority. All this redounds to the glory of God the Father.

Members of the church need to remind themselves that nothing in them merits praise. They are sinners doomed to die, and if it were not for the grace of God and His Christ, they would be nothing in the present and have nothing in the future. Since they owe everything to God, how can they be proud of anything?

It is the spirit of Satan that exalts self and makes a person selfish. But this grabbing spirit never leads to happiness, as many have found out. Thank God, Jesus is the light that gives light to every man,[10] and so He has implanted in everyone a desire for something better. When the goodness of God is presented in the clear light of revelation, then man is led to repentance.[11] Repentance will lead to conversion, and a man becomes a new creation in Christ. When this happens, a man is truly a member of the church. He can say with Paul, "The old has gone, the new has come!"[12]

He will recognize that "all this is from God, who reconciled us to himself through Christ and gave us the ministry of reconciliation."[13] He wants to cooperate with God in all His plans and purposes. All barriers of race and human differences cease to exist because Christ has broken down every barrier and made us one in Him.[14]

## The Importance of Unity

Jesus pointed out that without unity there can be no consistency and strength. When the Pharisees accused Him of casting out demons by the power inherent in the prince of demons, He said: "Every kingdom divided against itself will be ruined, and every city or household divided against itself will not stand."[15] He went on to draw the logical conclusion that if He was casting out demons by the power of Satan, then certainly Satan's kingdom could not stand. On the other hand, if He was driving out demons by the

Spirit of God, then the kingdom of God had come upon them.[16]

Matthew brings two opposing powers to view here. One is the power of Satan, which causes men to be blind and dumb. The other is the power of God, which releases men from captivity and pain. The church, as the center of God's activity, needs to be united if it is to accomplish one of its purposes, that of being a source of health and life to the community.

Furthermore Jesus pointed out that the unity of the church would help convince the world that the church was the object of God's love.

In human terms unity is often related to centralized control, strict supervision of every activity, discipline exercised to maintain order, unified leadership, and clearly identified goals that seem readily attainable. And some organizations have proved successful under such a regimen. But in such cases men have had to render blind obedience, authority has been strictly enforced, and discipline has been cruel and demanding.

All this is foreign to the church. It emphasizes individual responsibility under God, freedom of action under the Spirit, and the absence of a dictatorial stance on the part of church leaders. Nevertheless, when the church is united in action, cooperative in every venture, and determined to do what is right in God's sight regardless of consequences, then it becomes clear that the power of God is at work. Hence the church must claim the respect of the community in which it is placed.

Too often the unity that ought to characterize the church is lacking. People will follow human leadership rather than look to Christ for guidance. Paul was quick to show the church in Corinth that it was untrue to Christ when it was divided. "Is Christ divided?" he asked. Thus he showed that the church can only maintain unity when it acknowledges the headship of Christ.[17] No one must claim to be Christ's vicegerent on earth. No one must try to play the part of God in the church.

## Growth Into Unity

Someone has said that every living thing grows. We can expect, then, that the church, as a living organism, will constantly grow and develop.

Growth does not always mean an increase in size, but it does

imply advancing toward maturity, progressing to that point where
the organism reaches the acme of its performance.

Growth involves coordination. It means that the various parts
interact so as to achieve desired ends. In the world of nature as we
see it, sometimes growth can defeat the purposes of an organism.
Cancer is such a growth. And in the church sin sometimes causes
aberrations from the unity that ought to exist.

When sin exists in the church, there is only one solution: a
return to right principles. This will involve a study of the Word of
God. Peter wrote to the church members in his day and suggested:
"Like newborn babies, crave pure spiritual milk, so that by it you
may grow up in your salvation."[18] By "spiritual milk" he probably meant that which encourages spiritual growth. And since he
had just referred to the "living and enduring word of God" that had
been preached to them,[19] he very likely had this in mind. The figure
of speech of a baby suggests that the Christian needs to become
more mature as he fellowships in the church. He never considers
himself to have arrived, whether in knowledge or conduct.

Peter admitted that the Word of God is not always easy to
understand. He cited Paul's writings as an example! But he said
that the Word of God must not be distorted, as is done by ignorant
and unstable men. Instead the Christian must remain on his guard
and "grow in the grace and knowledge of our Lord and Savior
Jesus Christ."[20] This is positive growth, and it develops faith and
stability.

The danger always exists that some people will concern themselves with aspects of the Bible that will not promote growth in
faith. Paul directed Timothy in the following words: "Stay there in
Ephesus so that you may command certain men not to teach false
doctrines any longer nor to devote themselves to myths and endless
genealogies. These promote controversies rather than God's
work."[21] Like Peter, Paul wanted the church to grow positively in
love, peace, sincerity, a good conscience, and faith. We must avoid
those elements that cause confusion and division in the church.

## Barriers to Unity

Lack of spirituality among the members and leaders of the
church is the greatest cause of disunity and strife. When communion with God is missing, then people make up for their lack by

pursuing worldly aims by worldly methods. Paul put this thought boldly in the following terms: "The man without the Spirit does not accept the things that come from the Spirit of God, for they are foolishness to him, and he cannot understand them, because they are spiritually discerned."[22] William Barclay puts it very well: "A man who thinks that nothing is more important than the satisfaction of the sex urge cannot understand the meaning of chastity; a man who ranks the amassing of material things as the supreme end of life cannot understand generosity; and a man who has never a thought beyond this world cannot understand the things of God. To him they look mere foolishness."[23]

Mrs. White characterized many people today in the following words: "Today men are eagerly seeking for earthly treasure. Their minds are filled with selfish, ambitious thoughts. For the sake of gaining worldly riches, honor, or power, they place the maxims, traditions, and requirements of men above the requirements of God. From them the treasures of His word are hidden."[24] We need not limit this indictment to people outside the church. It could very well include baptized members, but they are members in name and not in spirit.

A unity achieved by compromise, where truth is suppressed or ignored, is a false unity. For this reason many efforts of the ecumenical movement fail. Ecumenical leaders seek for truths held in common, and they ask the members to mute their differences of opinion. But such an approach is bound to fail, because the Christian must remain faithful to the truth, the whole truth, and nothing but the truth. Anything short of this is disloyalty to the One who said that He was the truth.

Only in Christ can true unity exist.

## Footnotes

1. Ephesians 4:5
2. Acts 4:12
3. Acts 15:9
4. Galatians 2:20
5. Romans 6:3, 4
6. John 1:29
7. John 10:17, 18
8. John 12:27-33
9. Philippians 2:5-11
10. John 1:9
11. Romans 2:4
12. 2 Corinthians 5:17
13. 2 Corinthians 5:18
14. Ephesians 2:11-18
15. Matthew 12:25
16. Matthew 12:28

17. 1 Corinthians 1:10-17
18. 1 Peter 2:2
19. 1 Peter 1:23-25
20. See 2 Peter 3:14-18
21. 1 Timothy 1:3, 4
22. 1 Corinthians 2:14

23. Barclay, Wm., *The Letters to the Corinthians* (paperback), p. 28.
24. White, E. G., *Christ's Object Lessons* (Washington, D.C.: Review and Herald Publishing Association, 1941), p. 106.

Chapter 9

# Discipline for Life

Discipline in the sense of punishing the wrongdoer is not a popular word today. Parents are warned against strict control of their children in case it should lead to frustrations. The caution may be well taken, but the other extreme of permissiveness may not be helpful either. One needs to find that middle way between arbitrary control on the one hand and lack of guidance on the other.

The fact is that discipline in the proper sense implies more than a negative approach to wrongdoing. It means more than punishment. It includes the element of guidance, and it involves a relationship of love and concern. It is in this wider sense that the Bible refers to discipline. It is a responsibility both of the parent and of the church member. We need to discover what Biblical discipline really is so that we can respond positively when we are disciplined and so that we can exercise discipline understandingly when others are involved.

The objective of discipline is always remedial—a change of life-style. The changes desired are always for the individual's welfare, so that he may come to enjoy the blessings of life on earth and in heaven. Any other kind of discipline or control is pernicious.

Good discipline is always needed both in the home and in the church. Because of the human tendency to sin, children always need guidance and correction. For their own good they need to learn how to share their toys, how to behave properly in public, how to avoid street hazards, and how to get along with other people. In the same way the church member needs to learn what behavioral patterns are acceptable or not for their own good and for the good of others.

The Bible points out that God Himself is the Great Disciplinarian, and from Him we learn the principles of good discipline. For one thing, discipline is based on love. Only the one who loves supremely can exercise the right kind of discipline. Furthermore, certain principles of right and wrong always remain the same, regardless of time or race or culture. It is in harmony with those principles that proper discipline can be exercised.

Let us see if we can find in Scripture how God deals with us and how we ought to deal with one another in matters of guidance and correction.

### Divine Discipline

In Proverbs 3:11, 12 we read: ''My son, do not despise the Lord's discipline and do not resent his rebuke, because the Lord disciplines those he loves, as a father the son he delights in.'' The writer to the Hebrews quoted this passage of Scripture and emphasized that because we are God's sons He disciplines us.[1] If we were not sons, if God did not have a special concern for us, He would not bother to correct us. He would allow us to pursue our own wayward way and reap the consequences.

Discipline is never easy to take, because it involves pain and hardship. But such pain, like bitter medicine, needs to be endured because it ''produces a harvest of righteousness and peace for those who have been trained by it.''[2]

One blessing of divine discipline is that God always administers it in justice and mercy. It is always right for us. In this respect it differs from the kind of discipline we may have received from our earthly parents. They were not always wise enough to judge the situation adequately or to administer the punishment in proper doses. Some of us may harbor bitter memories of what our parents did to us. Yet we recognize that they thought they did what was right, and we honor and respect them for their concern on our behalf.

We shudder to think of the alternative. Suppose our parents had never corrected us but had let us go our own sweet way. What kind of selfish, willful creatures we would have become! Without guiding principles or evidence of love we would have been thrown to the mercy of a cruel and unrelenting world. We would have had to learn our lessons the hard way. We may know some people who have had just that kind of experience, and it should make us thankful that we have escaped such a fate.

The Book of Hebrews says that ''God disciplines us for our

good, that we may share in his holiness.''[3] If this is the objective of divine discipline, then we can never object to it. Rather, we welcome it and ask for grace to recognize in the experiences of life the way that God is dealing with us. We thank Him for His love. It is the height of ingratitude to reject what God is doing for our good.

It is interesting to note that God disciplines us to keep us humble so we may recognize that all good things come from Him. When we recognize our dependence on God, He can bless us, and He always provides us with all our needs.[4] Here the rich and affluent are sometimes tempted. They feel perfectly secure in their position, and hence their entrance into the kingdom is in jeopardy.[5]

## Self-discipline

Because man is a free moral agent he is expected to make his own decisions. In relation to God and his fellowmen he acts willfully, that is, he does not respond like a machine to situations. Instead, he weighs up the factors in a situation and decides to do one thing or another. In this sense he is responsible for his actions.

Since man has inherited a sinful nature, he needs to exercise self-control if he is not to be a creature of his nature and environment. He needs to watch his inherited tendencies toward evil and to control their urges. If he really takes seriously doing the right thing, he will do as Paul did when he said, ''I beat my body and make it my slave.''[6]

This attempted self-discipline does not always succeed, as Paul found by sad experience.[7] But Paul also found the secret of success in Jesus Christ our Lord. We need the power of God to overcome our wayward tendencies and our cultivated habits of evil. But first must come that decision to do the right and, if necessary, to keep our bodies under control.

Daniel affords an outstanding example of self-control. He and his companion resolved not to defile themselves with the royal food and wine.[8] It was rather embarrassing to do so because the king was extending to them a special favor. How could they refuse the royal fare? Would they not jeopardize their privileges?

Daniel decided that it would be better for him to remain true to the religious principles he had espoused than to yield to the exigencies of the moment and compromise his religious convictions. His whole life story reveals what happens to the person who determines to do the right regardless of the consequences.

Often in the matter of diet the Christian needs to exercise self-discipline. He does not eat food or drink beverages that he knows will harm his body. It is not a matter of quantity but of principle. He does not say, "A little will do me no harm." But by God's grace he totally abstains from all that is harmful. For him smoking or the use of drugs for highs is unthinkable.

Although the Bible gives specific guidance as to those foods that are proper to eat and those that are not,[9] Jesus pointed out the danger of being concerned only with material things. Matters of the heart need more attention, because "out of the heart come evil thoughts, murder, adultery, sexual immorality, theft, false testimony, slander."[10]

## Correcting Others

Regarding the work of disciplining others, a prominent Christian writer has said: "This work is the nicest, the most difficult, ever committed to human beings. It requires the most delicate tact, the finest susceptibility, a knowledge of human nature, and a heaven-born faith and patience, willing to work and watch and wait. It is a work than which nothing can be more important."[11]

This holds true not only for parents in the family situation but also for members in a church. Even though the church is called to holiness and the members are called to be saints, yet there are members who sin because of human weakness. In fact, we are all guilty of doing wrong, and the question immediately arises, what do we do to and for the wrongdoer?

One answer is perfectly clear: We cannot condone evil. But can we separate the sin from the sinner? To a certain extent this can be done, at least theoretically. We can love the sinner while not condoning his sin. But then again, it is difficult to differentiate between sinner and his sin because he is definitely implicated. Sometimes the only way to handle a sin is to deal with the sinner.

Another problem is that of judging. Motives are more important than actions, but motives remain hidden from view so far as we are concerned. So how can we judge truly? Obviously God is the only one who can judge fairly. Yet some sins are clear even to the human witness, and church members are not wholly released from recognizing sin and condemning it.

How does one go about correcting an obvious fault? The Bible is clear on this matter: The individual who knows of the fault must go directly to the person concerned and speak to him. [12]

It is not easy to go to a person directly and speak to him about his fault. It is much easier to talk to everyone else! But experience has shown that those who are willing to take the risks involved and handle the situation personally have had the greatest success in clearing up the damage and bringing about peace.

Of course, the one who undertakes to point out the fault must do so with great humility and tact. He makes sure that he is not as much at fault as anyone else. And if he is, he must be willing to confess his weaknesses and pray for forgiveness. There must be an obvious loving interest shown and a strong desire to build up and not tear down. Such a Christian spirit is rarely found, but when it exists, it is a force for reconciliation and for good.

Not all reconciliatory moves succeed. The one at fault may not be willing to see his mistake. In that case, the matter may have to be taken to a small group to handle or even to the church itself. But sin in a church member must not be neglected. Every effort must be made to bring about peace or reconciliation.

## Need for Disciplinary Action

The church must always guard against tolerating sin. To tolerate sin is to ignore the terribleness of sin, to forget what sin has done to the universe. Remember, sin caused our Lord to be crucified on Calvary. Therefore sin in the church must receive immediate and efficacious treatment.

It would seem that the church ought to be full of beautiful people. And so it is! But even beautiful people have their faults and make mistakes. We should not suppose that everyone in the church always does what is right. If we are so naive, we are in for a shock!

Yet I like to think that sinners in the church are better than sinners outside the church. But even in this I may be mistaken. Sin is sin, wherever it is committed. The only difference between the sinner in the church and the sinner in the world is that the former is willing to confess his sin and renounce it, whereas the latter tends to excuse his sin and holds on to it. Is that right?

Paul, writing to a young minister, Titus, warned him that he would find some bad members in the churches of Crete. He wrote:

"There are many rebellious people, mere talkers and deceivers, especially those of the circumcision group. They must be silenced, because they are ruining whole households by teaching things they ought not to teach—and that for the sake of dishonest gain."[13]

Have you seen such people in your church? Some people are good at talking, but they do very little else. They are quick to find fault, and they refuse to follow the appointed leader in the church, yet they have no alternative program of their own to offer. They are good at grumbling and complaining and making odious comparisons with other churches, but they do not lift a finger to improve the situation that they find so wrong.

Have you noticed that such people often come from a group that ought to know better, a privileged group? They are a pain in the neck for any church leader or member. No wonder Paul told Titus to silence such people. They are like the people Jesus referred to who "shut the kingdom of heaven in men's faces."[14] They do not go in themselves or let those who are trying to go in.

Paul instructed: "Rebuke them sharply."[15] Such people need summary treatment. It does no harm to deal clearly and decisively with matters that injure the church.

## Public Church Discipline

Most exercise of discipline should be private so as to safeguard the reputation of the people concerned. But when the sin is already well known, then the only remedy is to handle it publicly. It must be known that the church does not condone sin.

Peter's denial of his Lord was in the open, therefore his denial is well known today. But it is also well known that Jesus forgave him and reinstated him in the ministry.[16] This indicates that although sinning is serious and must be handled, it is not fatal when the sinner sincerely repents and returns to the Lord. The tragedy is that in many cases people refuse to forgive and forget. Some people demand, in righteous indignation, restitution or payment of a price.

There is nothing wrong in restitution or in producing "fruit in keeping with repentance."[17] Anyone who has truly repented will do this. But it is a different matter when people who judge want to exact payment or punishment. It is not for us to do what is the Lord's work. We must limit our actions to what is legitimate in man's sphere.

Paul heard of a serious case of sexual immorality in the church at Corinth. He was shocked that anyone in the church would commit a sin that even the pagans would shun. He was even more shocked to hear that no one in the church had done anything about it. Apparently no one felt even sorry that a member of the church had committed such an act. He had already judged the case in his own mind, and he wrote, "Hand this man over to Satan."[18]

The whole church assembled together to take this action "in the name of our Lord Jesus," with the power of the Lord Jesus being present. And the purpose was that the man's sinful flesh should be destroyed, but that the man's life might be spared as he turned to the Lord in repentance. This formal excommunication was drastic, but its purpose was therapeutic.

The Corinthian case was not the only one Paul dealt with in this way. Paul told Timothy that he had excommunicated two men who were blasphemers.[19] Once again the purpose was that they might learn not to continue in their way and be lost.

The church often fears to take drastic measures in a public way. However, the name of the church and its effectiveness can be seriously hampered if it harbors those who flagrantly sin. Furthermore, there must be no respect of persons or of the wealth that such persons may have. The church must stand for truth and not politics, for righteousness and not convenience.

## Justice and Mercy

Disciplinary action is usually based on justice. Is there a place in it for mercy?

Judgment is an essential phase of discipline. The acts and attitudes of someone are looked at and judged. There is an attachment of blame and an imposition of punishment. How, then, can mercy be shown?

Usually it is the attitude of the disciplinarian that counts. He may be harsh in his judgments, or he may be understanding. He can be cold or sympathetic. He can be austere or involved in the whole process. If he is a Christian, his justice will be tempered with his mercy.

Paul described the true Christian when he wrote to the church at Colosse: "Therefore, as God's chosen people, holy and dearly loved, clothe yourselves with compassion, kindness, humility, gentleness and patience. Bear with each other and forgive whatever grievances you may have against one another. Forgive as the Lord forgave you. And over all these virtues put on love, which binds them all together in perfect unity."[20] With such a spirit discipline can never go wrong.

However, discipline does not always demand punishment. Here is where mercy comes in. Repentance may be deep and real enough not to demand punishment to reinforce it. Sometimes the delinquent has already suffered enough in the process of investigation. To punish him further would only seem an injustice. Justice is not infringed when we show mercy. On the contrary, mercy can reinforce all those elements that make for reform. And if reform is the goal to be achieved, then mercy must have its place in the disciplinary process.

Some always assume that if punishment is not inflicted, the law may be slacked. Zealous for law and order, they are afraid that if retributive judgment does not reinforce the law, lawbreaking will be encouraged.

The Old Testament gives us an interesting example of this attitude.[21] Habakkuk noticed the violence in his community. He prayed that the Lord would do something about it. But apparently the Lord did not answer his prayer. The prophet complained that the Lord was tolerating wrong by such inaction. He went so far as to say the "law is paralyzed, and justice never prevails."[22] He felt that the wicked were having a heyday, while the righteous suffered at their hands.

God answered Habakkuk by telling him that He was doing something. It may not have been what the prophet expected, but it was action nevertheless. The Babylonians would invade the land.

God's ways are not our ways, and Habakkuk's real answer came in the unforgettable phrase, "the righteous will live by his faith."[23] In all our relations with other people, in disciplinary situations or not, we must be like God—just and merciful. Also we must let God be God and ever trust in Him.

## Footnotes

1. Hebrews 12:5
2. Hebrews 12:11

3. Hebrews 12:10
4. Deuteronomy 8:2-5

5. Mark 10:23-27
6. 1 Corinthians 9:27
7. Romans 7:21-25
8. Daniel 1:8
9. Leviticus 11
10. See Matthew 15:17-20
11. White, E. G., *Education* (Mountain View, California: Pacific Press Publishing Association, 1952), p. 292.
12. Matthew 18:15. This text seems to deal only with the one who has been wronged. But the principles of dealing with the situation surely apply to other cases. Ezekiel tells us that God appointed him a "watchman" with specific duties (compare Ezekiel 3:16-21). There is no reason why members of the church could not be watchmen in the same sense, as long as they carried out their duties with humility and godly grace. Mrs. White suggests that this is indeed the case. See *The Desire of Ages,* p. 355: "They [Christ's followers] are set as watchmen, to warn men of their peril."
13. Titus 1:10, 11
14. Matthew 23:13
15. Titus 1:13
16. John 21:15-19
17. Matthew 3:8
18. 1 Corinthians 5:5
19. 1 Timothy 1:20
20. Colossians 3:12-14
21. Habakkuk 1:2-4
22. Habakkuk 1:4
23. Habakkuk 2:4

Chapter 10

# Christian Concerns

What are some of the major concerns of the Christian? In this chapter we look at six of them and seek to understand them.

First and foremost is the concern to witness to the world of God's saving grace. When Jesus lived here on earth, He commissioned His disciples to "go and make disciples of all nations."[1] The Book of Acts records that on the day He ascended, Jesus informed His disciples: "You will receive power when the Holy Spirit comes on you; and you will be my witnesses in Jerusalem, and in all Judea and Samaria, and to the ends of the earth."[2] Thus the Christian and the church have a responsibility to the world. They are to represent Jesus and persuade men and women to accept God's unlimited favor.

Another primary concern is of that for truth. Christians believe that there is nothing so important to the mind and conscience as truth. They find this truth in Jesus Christ, who said that He was the way, the truth, and the life.[3] They also find it in the Bible, which witnesses to Jesus. For them the Bible is the Word of God. It is authoritative when it comes to matters of faith and practice. They must study the Word and make its truths available to the world.

A third concern is for health. The Christian recognizes the importance of the body. Unlike some people who consider the soul more important than the body, the Christian believes that health of body leads to health of mind and wholeness of spirit. The Bible has quite a bit to say about the care and importance of the body, and he seeks to follow its principles.

Three other concerns characterize the Christian:

1. He is loyal to the secular authorities that rule in his area. He recognizes that they are ordained of God to perform an important function in society. As a law-abiding citizen he knows that he can gain the respect of government officials and the members of his

community, and he thus can contribute to peace and prosperity.

2. He recognizes a responsibility for the poor and needy in his area and anywhere that disaster has struck. He cannot see his fellow human beings go hungry or naked when he himself has been blessed with the good things of life.

3. He is alive to the responsibility of passing on his religious heritage not only to his own children but to all children as potential members of Christ's kingdom. He knows that his Lord showed a special interest in children and drew important lessons from them.

Let us now look at these concerns in greater detail.

## Witnessing for Christ

Although Jesus commanded His disciples to go into all the world and preach the gospel, the Christian's concern to witness to and for his Lord arises out of an experience rather than a command. He has discovered some new truths and a new power that he must share. How can he be happy and not spread that happiness to others?

A brief glance at the early Christian church will reveal that the church members went everywhere preaching the Word.[4] The more they were persecuted, the more they preached. The more they were scattered, the more the gospel spread. At Antioch they preached not only to the Jews but also to the Greeks, and Luke commented: "The Lord's hand was with them, and a great number of people believed and turned to the Lord."[5]

What was the secret of this zeal, this constant witness? They had discovered that they no longer needed to be slaves of sin. When they learned that Jesus had come to die for their sins, they repented of their past, believed on the Lord Jesus, and were baptized. The old man was buried in baptism, and they had risen to "live a new life."[6] This experience was real and vivid. They could not keep it to themselves.

The early Christians had no doubt about the certainty of the gospel. All around them they saw miracles performed. The lame rose up and walked.[7] The sick were healed.[8] Even the dead were raised.[9] All this was done in the name of Jesus Christ. No wonder they talked about Him daily, extolling His virtues and presenting Him as the Saviour of the world.

Is the experience of the early church paralleled in our church today, in your personal experience? If not, why not?

The Christian concern today must be the same as that of the early church. We must all be ambassadors for Christ.[10] We are the agents God must use for reconciling the world to Himself. Paul used a beautiful expression to describe true Christians. He said they are "like stars in the universe" as they "hold out the word of life."[11]

I am afraid that today we tend to leave the work of witnessing and evangelism to individuals who are especially trained for the task. We look to the pastor to do this work. We remember that Paul told Timothy, a young minister, "Do the work of an evangelist."[12] Paul wrote to the Ephesians that "some" are evangelists.[13] We note that Philip was called an evangelist,[14] and rightly so because of the outstanding work of preaching he did in Samaria.[15] We forget that John the revelator reported: "The Spirit and the bride say, 'Come!' And let him who hears say, 'Come!' "[16] If we have heard the invitation to come and have tasted of the water of life, then it is for us to say to others: "Come, 'taste and see that the Lord is good.' "[17]

The Christian has a special reason for being concerned about the preaching of the gospel in all the world: Jesus cannot come until this work is completed.[18]

## Studying the Word

The Christian is concerned about the truth, the whole truth, and nothing but the truth. This expression may sound trite, but it is true nevertheless.

Where does the Christian find the truth? He finds it in Jesus Christ, who said of Himself, "I am the way and the truth and the life."[19] John in his witness about Jesus wrote: "The Word became flesh and lived for a while among us. We have seen his glory, the glory of the one and only Son, who came from the Father, full of grace and truth."[20] He contrasted Moses with Jesus and said, "For the law was given through Moses; grace and truth came through Jesus Christ."[21]

The Christian finds the truth also in the Bible, which witnesses to Jesus Christ. For him the Bible is the Word of God. Without the New Testament he would not know anything about Jesus. Without the Old Testament he would not know that Jesus came in fulfillment of prophecy. Without the Bible he would not know where he came from or where he is going. The Bible throws light on his present situation and gives him hope for the future. The Bible tells him how he should live and how God can help him achieve his goals. Without the Bible he would be lost in more ways than one.

The early church was closely attached to the person of Jesus and to the Scriptures. Of the first Christians we read that "they devoted themselves to the apostles' teaching."[22] Why the apostles' teaching? Because the apostles were eyewitnesses of the Lord. They had lived with Jesus, had heard His words, and had gone through the experiences of joy and sadness.[23] They were in a position to speak with authority about Him.

The apostles were also concerned with the Scriptures. Peter had appealed to Scripture when he preached the sermon at Pentecost.[24] Jesus was proved to be Lord and Christ because He fulfilled what the Old Testament prophets had prophesied about Him.

On a later occasion Luke reported of the Christians in Berea: "Now the Bereans were of more noble character than the Thessalonians, for they received the message with great eagerness and examined the Scriptures every day to see if what Paul said was true."[25] It is not a fault to study a matter for oneself. On the contrary, it makes for stability in the Christian experience. Would that more Christians would search the Scriptures for themselves! They would not then be carried away with every wind of doctrine.

The trouble with the world today is that there are many definitions of truth, many panaceas being offered for the world's ills. But the Christian knows that there is only one name under heaven whereby we must be saved—the name of Jesus.[26] There is only one truth, and that is what is revealed in the Word of God.

## Caring for the Body

The Christian is concerned about his body, his health, and his well-being. He finds in the Bible instructions as to what to eat and what not to eat.[27]

When God gave the children of Israel dietary instructions, He said that they were not to eat the flesh of certain animals.[28] Thus the pig, the rabbit, and sea creatures without both fins and scales are all considered unclean and not fit for human consumption. How many Christians today follow these injunctions?

Regarding the eating of pig's flesh, an Old Testament scholar has said: "Even under the most carefully supervised modern conditions of slaughtering and processing, the flesh of the pig is far more potentially dangerous as a source of infection than that of any of the other quadrupeds normally eaten for food. The pig is the intermediate host for several parasitic organisms, producing afflictions of varying severity."[29]

The New Testament does not say much about diet. Probably the Jews in the time of the apostles kept to their dietary principles even after they became Christians. However, when the Council at Jerusalem decided on what the Gentile Christians should observe, three of the four injunctions had to do with what was not to be eaten.[30]

The New Testament does emphasize the importance of the body. Paul urged the Christian to "flee from sexual immorality" because "he who sins sexually sins against his own body."[31] The body needs to be controlled. It is not evil in itself, but we are to dedicate it to God and not to evil purposes. In fact, it is a temple of the Holy Spirit. Therefore we ought to honor God in everything that we do with our bodies.[32] Paul went so far as to say, "If anyone destroys God's temple, God will destroy him; for God's temple is sacred, and you are that temple."[33]

The Christian cares about his body because he knows that the body underlies both spiritual and physical life. Only as he is true to his body is he true to his soul. Only as he is true to himself can he be true to God.

## Loyal to Authorities

The Christian is loyal to earthly authorities because he is loyal to God, who is behind all true authority. This does not mean that all authorities are right or legitimate. Too often they are not. But it does mean that the Christian supports law and order—not only for the sake of the people but also for the sake of the gospel. The church has everything to gain when there is order in society and everything to lose when there is chaos and anarchy.

How can the Christian promote law and order? He submits to rules and regulations. He recognizes that those who make the rules and regulations are not always good and honest men. But if God is in control of the nations, He is also in control of their rise and fall.

Not that everything done by government is right. But even in the worst of circumstances, God's name can be praised by Christians who stand up for truth and justice.

Both Paul and Peter emphasized the importance of the Christian's subjection to rulers and authorities.[34] Christians are to give honor where honor is due. They pay their taxes. They obey the laws and pray for those appointed to rule. The surprising thing is that the Christian does this even when the government is guilty of offenses against the church! Peter and Paul both experienced injustices at the hands of magistrates.

Why did the early Christian leaders equate Christianity with good citizenship? The question may be difficult to answer, but the wisdom, hopefully, is apparent.

Christians do not engage in insurrections and revolts because then their interests would be linked too closely with politics and worldly relationships—relationships that can only be temporary in nature. Furthermore, history has shown that rebellion involves bloodshed, destruction of property, and the injury of innocent people. Christians cannot, in good conscience, engage in such activities. Also very often the new regime is not much better than the old one. Human nature being what it is, greed and self-serving arise in any government.

Although Christians consider themselves only pilgrims in this world, they cannot deny their citizenship by birth or naturalization. They cannot opt out of the state in which they find themselves. Their church is also part of the society that makes up the state, and they cannot ignore the relationship. In addition, they enjoy many benefits as members of their society: the protection of their rights under the law; the protection of their property through a police force; services such as a water supply, a system of roads. The least they can do is to show their thankfulness by obeying the law.

## The Poor and Needy

The Christian shows concern for the underprivileged. He cannot enjoy the benefits that come to him if he knows that someone else is cold and hungry and needs help. As a steward of God's goods entrusted to him, he feels he cannot be true to God while he refuses to share with others when the need arises.

Poverty is a perennial phenomenon in all societies. Why does it exist? Sometimes it results from the greed and selfishness of individuals who take advantage of their fellowmen in order to make themselves rich. The Christian will avoid any such activity.

Sometimes an individual has brought the condition upon himself by foolishly handling his resources. If he has learned his lesson, he needs help to get back on his feet, and the Christian will happily help him.

Sometimes a disaster of nature strikes, such as a flood or a hurricane. The Christian will do all he can to help the injured and restore the damage.

Sometimes unforeseen tragedy comes, as when a fire or a famine breaks out. Sometimes the death of a loved one will take away the breadwinner of the family. There are all kinds of misfortunes and woes.

It is inherent in Christianity that we are all brothers and sisters, and so we help one another. True religion involves a living relationship with our fellowmen as well as a worshipful relationship with God. John put the matter very bluntly. "If anyone says, 'I love God,' yet hates his brother, he is a liar. For anyone who does not love his brother, whom he has seen, cannot love God, whom he has not seen."[35]

Some people feel self-righteous when they make large donations to the church. But if while doing this they neglect the needs of their kith and kin, they have forgotten the weightier matters of the law. Isaiah described the kind of religious expression that pleases God: "Is not this the kind of fasting that I have chosen: to loose the chains of injustice and untie the cords of the yoke, to set the oppressed free and break every yoke? Is it not to share your food with the hungry and to provide the poor wanderer with shelter—when you see the naked, to clothe him, and not to turn away from your own flesh and blood?"[36] Jesus roundly denounced the tradition of the Jews whereby a son could avoid caring for his aged parents by making a sacred donation to the temple.[37]

## Training the Youth

While children have a sacred obligation to honor their parents according to the fifth commandment, parents have no less an obligation to provide for the temporal and spiritual needs of their children.

The story of Abraham and his hospitality to three strangers attributes an interesting comment to God: "Then the Lord said, 'Shall I hide from Abraham what I am about to do? Abraham will surely become a great and powerful nation, and all nations on earth will be blessed through him. For I have chosen him, so that he will direct his children and his household after him to keep the way of the Lord by doing what is right and just, so that the Lord will bring about for Abraham what he has promised him.' "[38]

God decided to take Abraham into His confidence, as it were, on the basis that Abraham's posterity would become great and would be a means of blessing to others. But this future was guaranteed only on the basis that Abraham would "direct his children and his household after him." Only when parents effectively pass on to their children their religious heritage can the children become an honor. In fact, the fulfillment of God's promises to the parents depends on the fulfillment of their obligation to bring up their children in the way they should go.

Times have changed considerably since the days of the patriarchs. Modes of living, dress styles, and cultural habits have all changed. But one responsibility has not changed, that of giving the children and young people the training, example, and guidance that they need.

The disciples' attitude toward the children brought to Jesus for a blessing reflects that of many adults today.[39] They think that adult behavior and pursuits are more important than the needs of children. But Jesus rebuked such an attitude and told His disciples that children were an important element in God's kingdom. Children are future church members and parents. To neglect them is to neglect an important means of growth in the church and to weaken the church in succeeding generations.

No program costs the church more than that of educating its young people. But no budgetary cutting could cost the church more in the long run than that of reducing the effectiveness of Christian education. Some parents try to avoid the expense of sending their children to a church school. However, such a saving in money ends up in a loss of spiritual experience both for the parents and the children.

Being a parent involves sacrifice on behalf of the children. But all such sacrifice is an investment that can bring rich returns. Blessed are the parents whose children enter with them into the kingdom. Blessed are the children whose parents have introduced them to the joys of fellowship with Christ and doing His will. And blessed is the church that is full of members who praise God for the heritage of children and who make every provision for their welfare.

## Footnotes

1. Matthew 28:19
2. Acts 1:8
3. John 14:6
4. Acts 8:4, KJV
5. Acts 11:21
6. Romans 6:4
7. Acts 3:6-10
8. Acts 5:12-16
9. Acts 9:36-42
10. 2 Corinthians 5:20
11. Philippians 2:15, 16
12. 2 Timothy 4:5
13. Ephesians 4:11
14. Acts 21:8
15. Acts 8:5-8
16. Revelation 22:17
17. Psalm 34:8
18. Matthew 24:14
19. John 14:6
20. John 1:14
21. John 1:17
22. Acts 2:42
23. Acts 1:21
24. Acts 2:14-40
25. Acts 17:11
26. Acts 4:12
27. Genesis 9:4
28. Leviticus 11
29. Harrison, R. K., *Introduction to the Old Testament* (Grand Rapids, Michigan: William B. Eerdmans Publishing Co., 1969), p. 605.
30. Acts 15:20
31. 1 Corinthians 6:18
32. 1 Corinthians 6:19, 20
33. 1 Corinthians 3:17
34. Romans 13:1-7; 1 Timothy 2:1, 2; Titus 3:1; 1 Peter 2:13-17
35. 1 John 4:20
36. Isaiah 58:6, 7
37. Mark 7:9-13
38. Genesis 18:17-19
39. Matthew 19:13-15

Chapter 11

# Organized for Efficiency

Organization can be a blessing or a curse. It is a curse when it stifles individual initiative, takes away personal responsibility, and becomes an end in itself. But it is a blessing when it clearly defines areas of responsibility so that there is no overlapping of effort, when it provides for wide counsel among the members, and when it makes for adequate planning and distributes responsibility for the carrying out of proper projects.

Jesus pointed out that it was the better part of wisdom to plan a tower before starting to build it. To begin a task and not to complete it because of a failure to adequately prepare is a shame.[1] The same applies to a ruling monarch who finds himself faced with the possibility of a war. If he cannot meet and defeat his enemy, he had better seek terms of peace and reconciliation.[2]

All this seems to be part of worldly wisdom, but Jesus pointed out that what was wise for a secular organization can also be wise for the church. The individual member must sit down and count the cost of discipleship before he makes his decision. Such a decision is not only costly but it would also be a shame for him to embark upon a project that he cannot complete. And the same principle applies to the church. A church must have that kind of organization that ensures a wise approach to problems and projects, so that no one will be embarrassed by inefficient planning.

Organize for efficiency. That is the secret of success. It is not organization per se that counts. Rather, structure must contribute to the effective pursuit of function. One may be overorganized, just as one may be underorganized. The church must seek that kind of organization which helps to achieve its purpose. When such an organization is attained, the church can operate efficiently.

Secular agencies, whether they be in business or manufacturing or government often use the word *efficiency*. Any self-respecting corporation will seek efficiency, because without it the corporate body cannot meet its goals. The same is true of the church. Only when everyone in the church—officer or layman—fulfulls his function efficiently is the church efficient as a whole.

Does it sound too worldly to think of the church as a body that needs to be organized for productivity? Do you feel that since God is in control of the church one does not need to be concerned about organization?

It is true that the church is in a special sense the sphere of God's activity on the earth. If He is not in control, the church is not a church. But a brief glance at the way God has revealed Himself will show that God is a God of order. Consider the process of creation. Everything followed in logical order, and everything was efficiently produced. It is sin that has brought about confusion and disarray, not only in the physical universe around us but also in man's constitution. Mrs. White puts it strongly. "Through sin the whole human organism is deranged, the mind is perverted, the imagination corrupted. Sin has degraded the faculties of the soul. Temptations from without find an answering chord within the heart, and the feet turn imperceptibly toward evil."[3]

### A God of Order

In Creation God brought order out of chaos.[4] After He had created man, He placed him in charge of the earth to subdue it and to rule over the animals.[5] Thus there were to be law and order. Only after the fall of man do we read of a curse and enmity and strife and pain and domination and thorns and death. In the first family there were rebellion and murder.

But God has wanted to restore order. He destroyed the antediluvians because they had set their minds on evil, and then He promised Noah that there would be a regular succession of the seasons.[6] Regarding the church, Mrs. White has well said: "Christ designs that heaven's order, heaven's plan of government, heaven's divine harmony, shall be represented by His church on earth."[7] And then again: "On the church has been conferred the power to act in Christ's stead. It is God's instrumentality for the preservation of order and discipline among His people."[8] Furthermore, "He who despises the authority of the church, despises the authority of Christ Himself."[9] Thus God's order is to prevail within.

Unfortunately, because of the human element in the church, harmony and order have not always characterized the churches. This was the case in the Corinthian church, and Paul sent them a strong letter of rebuke. Regarding the services in the church, he said that "everything should be done in a fitting and orderly way."[10]

Paul offered specific counsel regarding worship procedures in the church, since "God is not a God of disorder but of peace."[11] There was not to be a babble of voices, but one speaker should hold the floor for a time. Whatever was said should be intelligible to the listeners. If someone spoke in a foreign tongue, someone else should translate. If no translator was available, then the speaker who could use only a foreign language should remain silent. The objective of worship was that everyone should be instructed and encouraged, and any activity that did not contribute to this end should be discouraged.[12] All this was not a matter for one church but for all the churches. And if there were men of God around, they would recognize that what Paul had outlined was in harmony with the Spirit of God.

Paul also referred to women and their part in the church. We should understand this in terms of the customs in Paul's day. Undoubtedly similar circumstances may still prevail in some parts of the world today. Not everywhere can women lead out in the church without causing misunderstandings and stumblings. Once again, the objective of all worship must be kept in mind—that which will edify and bring harmony.

## Order in Israel

In the history of the children of Israel under Moses we read of a very important principle of decentralization and delegation of authority in organization.[13] A religious leader might undertake to do too much for his congregation. Moses did. But it was also a mark of good leadership that Moses recognized the wisdom of his father-in-law and agreed to appoint others who could guide and counsel the people. Here the principle of efficiency came into play. More work was done in less time.

Nothing is gained when a church leader overworks. On the contrary, his loss of health will mean a loss of further service to the church. He is wiser to invite others to join him in carrying the various responsibilities that lie on his shoulders. In this way the people are served better and longer.

One of the remarkable aspects of God's economy with the children of Israel was the great detail with which every aspect of worship and conduct was specified. One cannot read the Book of Leviticus without noticing the repetition of such words as, "The Lord said to Moses." Another frequent phrase is, "These are the regulations." The Book of Exodus reveals the details God provided for the tabernacle. Even the garments worn by the priests were described in detail. Furthermore, God said that He had chosen certain individuals to do some of the intricate construction, and for this purpose He had given them a measure of the Holy Spirit.[14] Why all this detail and concern for exactness? Is it not because the children of Israel were to be separate and distinct from the peoples around? As God's people they were to worship in God's ordained way. The church should not ape any of the forms of worship that there may be in the world. The church must worship in a pattern acceptable to God. Its worship will have meaning in every aspect.

The importance of strictly following the pattern that God has set for worship is brought out very clearly in the story of Nadab and Abihu. When they offered strange fire, they were immediately consumed by fire.[15] Moses instructed the family not to mourn for them, because in so doing they would be condoning evil.

Summary judgment fell on Uzzah because he dared touch the ark when the oxen stumbled.[16] We may not fully understand why such a severe punishment should be meted out in such a case, but one truth stands out clearly: No one can disobey God with impunity. It always behooves us to find out God's will and to do it.

## God's Army

The church has been likened to an army because of the gigantic struggle going on between Christ, representing all that is good, and Satan, representing all that is evil. The church is in the midst of this struggle, and every member plays a part. Paul admonished Christians to put on the whole armor of God.[17] Only in this way can they withstand the powers of evil and be able to stand victorious in the end.

The figure of speech of an army is an apt one for the church not only because of the fight of faith against evil that goes on every day but also because of the organization in the army that makes for efficiency. From the five-star general down to the buck private there is a line of authority that must be respected. Let us note some of the parallels between army and church:

1. Every army has its supreme commander, and the church has its Supreme Head, Jesus Christ. It is the place of the commander to know what to do and when. He gives the orders. Likewise the church must always keep in touch with its Head if it wishes to function effectively in the world.

2. Just as every soldier has to put up with hardship and inconveniences in his line of duty, so the church member must devote himself wholly to the teachings and activities of the church even though these may involve sacrifice.

3. The soldier knows that he has been called away from civilian duties to engage in a special line of duty, and he must give himself wholly over to the demands of army life. Likewise the church member knows that he cannot mix worldly activities and pleasure with the responsibilities he carries in the church. He serves only one master—his Lord Jesus Christ.[18] It is not surprising, therefore, to find that one of the most popular hymns says: "Onward, Christian soldiers!/Marching as to war,/With the cross of Jesus/Going on before."[19]

Nevertheless, it must be made clear that the warfare in which the Christian takes part is a spiritual warfare. He does not take up the sword in a literal sense. He does not fight with people in a physical sense. He fights as did Paul the good fight of faith.[20] He is concerned about truth and righteousness and a vindication of God's character. Such a fight demands his intellect, his reasoning powers, and a stand for the truth though the heavens fall! Such a fight can make greater demands on his courage and stamina than a physical war would. But it can also bring with it greater satisfaction and greater rewards.

## Disciples on a Mission

One of the striking truths of the New Testament is the contrast between the small number of disciples on the one hand and the immense proportions of the Great Commission of the other. To the uninitiated it is a mystery how so few could be expected to do so much. Yet Jesus not only called individuals to follow Him, but He also sent them forth with a task to accomplish. He not only gave them a work to do, but He also gave them unusual powers that enabled them to come back with the exhilaration of success.[21]

Jesus gave His disciples detailed instructions as to what to do, and He sent them in pairs. This suggests that the church should not undertake a mission without clear direction. Church members must have the skills necessary to do what needs to be done, otherwise they would be little more than a rabble and would accomplish as little! Church activity must always be well thought out and planned down to the smallest detail, because only in this way can it truly represent the God of order.

It is not without significance that Jesus sent out the disciples two by two. Not only are two heads better than one in approaching a problem or seeking a solution, but also no one has sufficient wisdom to undertake the task on his own. There is always a danger in allowing one person to solve a matter, because his experience is limited. Some people are very confident in their ability. They often want to take the lead in church matters, but their very self-confidence is a danger. Experience has shown that when two or more engage in a church activity, greater success will follow.

There is mutual strength in companionship. One will encourage another, or, if necessary, one will prevent the other from being rash. There is wisdom in mutual counsel. That is why a group should always consider church matters before action is taken. Thus the church will not be molded by the characteristics of one person. Instead, it will represent the combined wisdom of the whole.

Mrs. White attributed much of the success of the Waldensian church to the fact that "the missionaries went out two and two, as Jesus sent forth His disciples. With each young man was usually associated a man of age and experience, the youth being under the guidance of his companion, who was held responsible for his training, and whose instruction he was required to heed. These colaborers were not always together, but often met for prayer and counsel, thus strengthening each other in the faith."[22]

It is not numbers that give success but dedication to God's work. The experience of Gideon offers an outstanding example of this truth. Not with thirty-two thousand men did he gain the victory over the enemy, but with a fearless and dedicated three hundred.[23]

## Need for Structure

When I was much younger, I once told my sister that she could not go outside to play. She looked up at me defiantly and said, "You are not my Mummy!" As far as I remember she went outside and played with impunity.

My younger sister was telling me that she recognized her mother's authority in directing her activities, but she did not recognize mine. And that was it.

The recognition of authority is important in any society. It matters little what the pattern of authority may be. It may be patriarchal or a benevolent monarchy. It may be theocratic or democratic. The point is not so much the form as it is the efficiency in meeting the needs of the people. Down through history there have been many forms of government. All have had their weaknesses and failures, but all have had some measure of success in providing the order and discipline needed in society.

The church must also have its structure. Arguments may be put forward for one form of church polity or another, but the fact is that any polity, however perfect in theory, may fail because of the human element. It is therefore not the form but the practice that is important.

Some churches have an episcopal form of government. Others do not use the terms *bishop* or *archbishop* but use the word *president*. Some have priests leading out in the ministry for the people. Others have elders. Some have a papal form of hierarchy applying to the whole church, whereas others prefer a congregational form of organization whereby each church is autonomous in its administration. Still others opt for a representational form of church order. Does the name really matter?

Of course, a name does have its influence, and that is why one branch of the church calls itself Presbyterian. It thereby says that it does not want to see a monarchical bishop exercising personal authority in the church. Obviously a form of organization that unites the various churches into one is preferable to one that emphasizes differences. But in the end, it is not the *form* that counts so much as the *practice,* and the practice should involve the whole church. This suggests that the representational form of church order is the best. Do you know how your church is organized and how it functions?

When a recognized structure works effectively in the church there is peace and harmony. The church becomes like a body in which every organ does its work. The body can do its work without thinking all the time of what the heart or the kidney or any other organ ought to be doing. That was why Paul left Titus in Crete. He wanted the churches to be organized for efficiency.[24] The work of the church includes many administrative details, such as the time and place of meeting, the collection and distribution of funds, the order of service, prayer for the sick, and other duties. Someone needs to help coordinate the program.

### Overorganization

Is it possible for a church to be overorganized?

Unfortunately, the answer to this question is yes! Church services can be so formalized that the spirit of worship gets lost in the ritual. Prayers may be merely read. ''Worship'' may be little more than a series of genuflections. Going through the motions may be all that is required of anyone, because everything has been decided beforehand.

Reacting to the obvious formality of certain kinds of worship, some church members go to the other extreme of not making any preparations at all. They want the Spirit to guide them, and so they leave everything to the last minute for so-called guidance of the Spirit.

Much as one may sympathize with the emphasis on the importance of God's presence in the services, one must express a word of caution against a leadership that scorns adequate preparation for a church service. The preacher must carefully consider what he will say to his congregation. He cannot waste their time with thoughts and expressions of little moment. He needs to organize his thoughts, choose his words carefully, and present his points convincingly. No one can do this ''off the cuff,'' however gifted he may be as a speaker.

Any part of the church service that requires the cooperation of two or more people should be adequately rehearsed. This certainly applies to the choir or to the musical group. Inadequate preparation spells disaster. But the same applies to the work of the deacons, where coordination is likewise important. If the church serves a hospitality dinner, it should be well planned.

On the other hand, the church service is not to be a play that is rehearsed and then presented to the congregation. Prayer must be communion with God and not a recitation. While the subject of the offering appeal should be well studied, the appeal itself should come from the heart. The Scripture reading should be handled reverently, because it represents the spoken Word of God.

No one can be too prepared for his part in a church service. But there is always the danger of losing the spirit of worship. Organization may become an end in itself, and if it does so, then it ceases to serve the purposes of the church.

## Footnotes

1. Luke 14:28-30
2. Luke 14:31, 32
3. White, E. G., *The Ministry of Healing* (Mountain View, California.: Pacific Press Publishing Association, 1942), p. 451.
4. Genesis 1:1, 2
5. Genesis 1:28
6. Genesis 8:22
7. White, E. G., *Gospel Workers* (Washington, D.C.: Review and Herald Publishing Association, 1915), p. 443.
8. *Ibid.,* pp. 501, 502
9. *Ibid.,* p. 503
10. 1 Corinthians 14:40
11. 1 Corinthians 14:33
12. 1 Corinthians 14:26-40
13. Exodus 18:18-26
14. Exodus 31:2
15. Leviticus 10:1, 2
16. 1 Chronicles 13:9, 10
17. Ephesians 6:11-17
18. 2 Timothy 2:3, 4
19. *Church Hymnal,* No. 360, first stanza
20. 2 Timothy 4:7
21. Mark 6:12, 13; Luke 9:6
22. White, E. G., *The Great Controversy* (Mountain View, California: Pacific Press Publishing Association, 1911), p. 71.
23. Judges 7:2-15
24. Titus 1:5

Chapter 12

# Servant Leaders

Principles of good leadership apply in all forms of society, including the church. However, the leader in the church must be more than a leader. He must also be a servant.

There is an apparent contradiction between being a leader and being a servant. How can one lead and serve at the same time? Does not the leader occupy a position of honor? Does he not command and expect others to obey him? How, then, does he occupy the lower position of being a servant, of receiving orders and fulfilling them?

In order to resolve the paradox we must look at Jesus. He supremely represented the principle of leadership that serves. His whole life was one of service. And at the same time He was the greatest leader the world has ever seen.

Even at the age of twelve He occupied a commanding position. There we see Him "in the temple courts, sitting among the teachers, listening to them and asking them questions. Everyone who heard him was amazed at his understanding and his answers."[1] He had applied Himself to the study of God's Word. He was listening and learning. He was also asking questions and drawing conclusions. He was independent in His thinking. He was expressing His personality, and people were amazed. Even His parents were surprised. Yet He humbly returned to Nazareth and dutifully obeyed His parents. The Gospel of Luke reports that He "grew in wisdom and stature, and in favor with God and men."[2]

Leaders in the church would do well to emulate Jesus in studying and understanding the Scriptures. At the same time they should never take pride in their accomplishments but should occupy their position humbly. In this way they would win both the favor of God and of man—a vertical and horizontal relationship in perfect balance.

During the last hours of Christ's earthly ministry, He took off His outer garment, wrapped a towel around His waist, and set about to wash His disciples' feet. He was the Lord and Master, and yet He undertook the work of a servant. Why did He do this? He explained His action in these words: "I have set you an example that you should do as I have done for you." Then He added: "Now that you know these things, you will be blessed if you do them."[3]

Jesus' example of leadership differed greatly from that found in the world. Leadership in the church means humble service. It means leading for the sake of others and not for the sake of one's own aggrandizement. It means a life of sacrifice and not a life of amassing wealth or power. It may mean losing one's temporal life, but it means gaining eternal life. John expressed what God has done for us and therefore what we ought to do for others in these words: "Jesus Christ laid down his life for us. And we ought to lay down our lives for our brothers."[4]

## A Serving Master

Jesus summed up His life purpose by saying that "the Son of Man did not come to be served, but to serve, and to give his life as a ransom for many."[5] This was obvious not only in the death that He died but in the life that He lived.

Everything that Jesus did served a specific need, and that need was in someone else and not in Himself. In the wilderness He refused to satisfy His hunger by turning stones into bread,[6] but in Cana of Galilee He turned water into wine because a family was embarrassed by a lack of sufficient wine to entertain guests.[7] He healed the sick and the palsied, the lepers and the blind, because men and women everywhere needed relief from their pain and suffering. One person had already spent all she had on doctors but without improvement. In fact her condition had worsened![8] Jesus was sometimes accused of spending His time with sinners, but He decisively replied: "It is not the healthy who need a doctor, but the sick."[9] He was always found where He was needed.

Jesus pointed out that the supreme test of a person's love was his willingness to lay down his life for his friend.[10] But He also made it clear that He Himself laid down His life. It was not taken away from Him. His death did not occur because of circumstances over which He had no control. On the contrary, He it was who had authority to lay it down and to take it up again.[11] This makes Jesus, the Lamb of God that takes away the sin of the world, a willing sacrifice. In this respect He also fulfilled the role of the suffering servant brought out so poignantly by Isaiah: "He was pierced for our transgressions, he was crushed for our iniquities, . . . and by his wounds we are healed."[12]

Because Jesus has set us an example, we should follow in His footsteps. Not that any of us can come close to the standard of sacrificial service that He set. But at least we can consider Paul's appeal to present our bodies as "living sacrifices."[13] We can seek to place our lives in the furrow of the world's needs. We can pray with Francis of Assisi: "Lord, make me an instrument of your peace. . . . Grant that I may not so much seek to be consoled, as to console; to be understood, as to understand; to be loved, as to love; for it is in giving that we receive; it is in pardoning that we are pardoned, and it is in dying that we are born to eternal life."[14] We can express our dedication to Christ's cause and to the church by making ourselves slaves to everyone, not seeking our own good but the good of all.[15]

## Chosen to Serve

As the church grew and developed in Jerusalem, it soon became obvious that the twelve apostles could not alone assume all the responsibilities devolving upon church leadership. Just as Moses could not singlehandedly judge the children of Israel in the wilderness, so the Twelve could not do for the church all that was necessary.

Crises may arise in any organization. But the crisis is not the main event. It is the way the crisis is met and the problem is solved that determines the effectiveness of the organization. In the case of the growing church in Jerusalem some people felt neglected in the distribution of food.[16]

The problem in the church took on racial or nationalistic lines. The Greeks complained about neglect from the non-Greek elements in the church. It is easy for the church, interracial in character, to become suddenly conscious of racial differences! The result is separation and division. Every member of the church must beware lest the enemy sow racial discord that will cause division where there needs to be harmony.

The problem in the early church was solved immediately by taking necessary organizational steps. There was no question about the impropriety of unequal distribution of assistance to the members. There was no question of impugning the honesty of the existing leadership. There was just an obvious need for more leaders. Some would concern themselves with one phase of church activity, and others would care for other needs. Both would serve the church differently but equally.

It is important to note that the whole church was involved in the problem and that the whole church took part in the solution. It is unfortunate when church members leave it to church leaders to solve all problems, or when church leaders feel that they do not need to consult the church members when they face a problem. Everyone has a vested interest in the church, and the wisdom of a larger group is safer than the prognostications of the few. Every faithful member of the church has a direct line to the Holy Spirit, who should decide all important matters in the church.

Some suggest that devoting oneself to prayer and the ministry of the Word is more important to the church than deacons. Such thinking has led to concepts of a hierarchy in the church, of one office being higher than another. A study of the qualifications needed for being a deacon[17] and of the lives of Stephen and Philip soon reveals that comparisons of this kind do more harm than good. God calls both ministers and laymen to serve the church in the way the Holy Spirit has endowed them. The church is basically led by the Holy Spirit, and not by men.

### Gifts for Service

Members of the church are gifted people. Some have more gifts than others, as Jesus taught in the parable of the talents.[18] But even the person who has only one talent is as responsible for using his gift as is the five-talent person. Jesus leaves no excuse for saying, "I am not as smart as the other person. Therefore I shall let the other person do the work."

It is a privilege to have talents, but it is not a matter for pride or arrogance. All talents are given. Even the opportunities to develop them are given. Talents are a responsibility because they are gifts to be used only in God's service and only to God's honor.

Writing to the Ephesians, Paul made it perfectly clear that all talents are gifts of the Holy Spirit. These gifts, he stated, are "to prepare God's people for works of service."[19] The goal to be reached in the church is that all God's people shall be thoroughly prepared to serve God according to the talents that they have received.

Does this concept prevail in our church today? Unfortunately in many churches the members are merely spectators. The ministers do all the work. A dichotomy has developed between clergy and laymen. The clergy take the lead in all spiritual activities. The laymen may be asked to engage in menial matters (and certainly to make a financial contribution to support the church), but that is as far as their responsibilities stretch.

But there has been a growing realization in recent years that the church can never accomplish its task if it depends wholly on the activities of the minister. Every member must engage in personal witness if this gospel of the kingdom is to go to all the world in this or any generation.

The experience of the early church reveals this to be true, and the teaching of the apostles certainly indicates that all are called to work for God. Each must serve in his own way and in his own environment. The thought that the church can be divided into two separate compartments, the clergy and the laity, is a false one. The church is not only to engage in preaching and teaching but also in practical service, such as that performed by the Good Samaritan. In this way people can come to know God's love and yield their lives in service to Him.

### Leadership Roles

We have just seen that every member of the church is gifted in order to serve. He is a servant-leader in his community. But Paul did not leave leadership roles vague or uncertain. He gave a list that is worthy of study, because it indicates the kind of activity that we should be able to recognize both inside and outside the church.

"But to each one of us grace has been given as Christ apportioned it. . . . It was he who gave some to be apostles, some to be prophets, some to be evangelists, and some to be pastors and teachers."[20] It would seem from this language that God gives the *person* as well as the gift.

There is a difference between a profession in the world and an office in the church. A profession may be chosen, but a ministry is conferred. One may choose to be a lawyer or a dentist, train for the work, and be successful at it. But one may not choose to be an apostle or a prophet or an evangelist or a pastor or a teacher. One must be chosen for the task and empowered to do it. In the church, God is in control. If God is not in control, then there is no church, even though an organization may call itself a church.

We generally consider that apostleship is the highest office that can be held in the church. We think immediately of the twelve apostles. But Paul also called himself an apostle,[21] and few would want to dispute his claim. The New Testament also calls Barnabas and James, the Lord's brother, apostles.[22] Not many churches use the name today for any of their leaders, but since the word *apostle* really means "one who is sent," it would be possible to think of duly accredited missionaries as apostles. Their work is certainly important in the outreach activity of the church.

The word *prophet,* etymologically, means "one who speaks for God." In Old Testament times there were many prophets, whose prophesyings were both oral and written. In New Testament times we read of Philip who had four daughters who prophesied.[23] This reminds us that prophets were not always men. Jesus warned against false prophets in the last days, indicating that there would be the gift of prophecy in the church but that one must differentiate between the true and the false. It is very important for the church to be guided by its true prophets.

An evangelist brings the Good News to those who have not heard it. His concern is to work outside the church, to bring disciples into the church. By contrast, the pastor and teacher work inside the church, building up the members in the faith and helping them meet their obligations spiritually. The pastoring and teaching ministries are apparently complementary, the one hardly sufficing without the other.

### Elders and a Council

One officer in the church—the elder—is mentioned again and again in the New Testament.

As the name implies, an elder was an older person and, presumably because of his age, more experienced and more knowledgeable. As a respected member of the community, he was sought after for counsel. As a long-standing and faithful member of the church, he would be looked upon as a leader and highly regarded if he was nominated in some official way to serve as "elder" of the church. Paul and Barnabas, after visiting churches in Asia Minor, "appointed elders for them in each church and, with prayer and fasting, committed them to the Lord in whom they had put their trust."[24]

Peter wrote to the elders "as a fellow elder" and suggested that they were to be "shepherds of God's flock" and to serve as "overseers."[25] The term *overseer,* or *bishop,* was used by Paul in writing to Titus and instructing him to "appoint elders in every town."[26] Apparently the early church used the titles of elder and bishop interchangeably. Only later did the office of a bishop assume a higher place than that of an elder. Because of the abuse of the office of bishop, some Christian churches today refuse to have leaders in their churches called bishops, although some churches still use the title.

Paul said that Timothy had had the "body of elders" lay their hands on him in a form of ordination.[27] Hence the church today ordains its elders in a special ceremony that sets them apart as spiritual leaders. James pointed out that they may be called upon to offer special prayers for the sick.[28] They were men of God who lived exemplary lives, as is indicated by the qualifications that they had to meet.[29]

The elders no doubt could and did meet together to discuss mutual problems. In Acts 15:1-35 we read of an important occasion when apostles and elders met with delegates from the church at Antioch to decide how far, if at all, Gentile converts to Christianity were to be Judaized. Distinct differences of opinion existed. Speeches were made on both sides of the issue. The assembly remained hushed while Paul and Barnabas recounted the miracles God had performed during their ministry. Then James, as the presiding officer, summarized the situation as he saw it. We read that the apostles and elders "with the whole church" solved the problem together. The letter which was then sent to Antioch contained the phrase: "It seemed good to the Holy Spirit and to us."[30] Here is a picture of the church in action. There was mutual counsel. Everyone was involved. The Holy Spirit was evidently leading in the decision that had been taken.

## False Leaders

It must not surprise the church member if sometimes false prophets and false leaders enter the church. Jesus warned against the first kind as making false claims and against the second as existing even in His day.[31] We need always to be able to distinguish between the true and the false.

To be on the positive side, let us look at the qualifications of good leadership in the church:

1. A person is recognized as a good leader in the church when what he says is usually positive, wise, and good. He speaks with the authority of knowledge and experience. He does not lobby for leadership, but the church listens to him and recognizes him for what he is—a loyal, dedicated member of the church who perceives matters as they really are and who offers possible solutions where others can see only perplexities.

2. A leader has a decisive outlook. He does not hesitate to express an opinion, even if he should be in the minority. He is not arrogant or proud, but he is honest, quick to acknowledge a mistake, and ready to change his mind when the evidence is convincing. He is firm in his convictions but respectful of the view of his opponents.

3. He is generally optimistic and enthusiastic about good causes. He works hard and cooperates with others in achieving success. People like to work with him because he gives credit where credit is due.

4. Possible failure does not intimidate him. He has confidence in God's leading, so he willingly undertakes responsibilities for the church. He knows that the God who has called him will also see him through.

5. He can communicate his ideals, and people follow him. But more importantly, he is filled with the Holy Spirit. He is anxious to do only what is right and to follow God's leading. He recognizes that it is not for him to assume leadership. Rather, he accepts it if it is offered.

Who should never be called upon to lead out in the church?

1. The person who feels that he is always right and that the current leadership is always wrong.

2. The one who seeks leadership for the name and prestige that it will give him.

3. The person who teaches un-Biblical doctrines.

4. The one who does not have the respect of his wife and children, whose homelife is falling apart.

5. The person who has the law but not the grace of God in his heart.

Now would you like to add some more characteristics on your own?

## Footnotes

1. Luke 2:46, 47
2. Luke 2:52
3. John 13:15, 17
4. 1 John 3:16
5. Matthew 20:28
6. Matthew 4:3, 4
7. John 2:1-10
8. Mark 5:26
9. Matthew 9:12
10. John 15:13
11. John 10:17, 18
12. Isaiah 53:5
13. Romans 12:1
14. *Guideposts Trilogy* (Carmel, New York: Guideposts Associates, Inc., 1962), p. 197.
15. 1 Corinthians 9:19; 10:33
16. Acts 6:1
17. Acts 6:3; 1 Timothy 3:8-13
18. Matthew 25:14-30
19. Ephesians 4:11, 12
20. Ephesians 4:7-11
21. 1 Corinthians 9:1
22. Acts 14:3, 4; Galatians 1:19
23. Acts 21:8, 9
24. Acts 14:23
25. 1 Peter 5:1, 2
26. Titus 1:5-9; cf. Acts 20:17, 28, where elders are also called bishops (see footnote).
27. 1 Timothy 4:14
28. James 5:14
29. 1 Timothy 3:1-7
30. Acts 15:28
31. Read Matthew 23 for a description of the Pharisees and the teachers of the law, who certainly preached but never practiced what they preached!

# Chapter 13

# Speeding Our Lord's Return

Toward the close of His earthly ministry, Jesus shocked His disciples by telling them that He would soon leave them. But they were not to let their hearts be troubled. The trust that they had in God, whom they had never seen, could be translated into a trust in Him, whom they would not see for some time to come. Furthermore, the absence was necessary in order "to prepare a place" for them.[1]

The announcement came as a shock, but it was also a promise. For Jesus was not only telling them of a departure but also of a return. "I will come back," He said, "and take you to be with me."[2] Jesus was telling them that there would be a separation, but there would also be a reunion in time. Then Jesus and His disciples would live happily together forevermore.

The disciples were naturally interested in the time of Jesus' promise to return. So soon after the Resurrection they asked: "Lord, are you at this time going to restore the kingdom to Israel?"[3] But Jesus discouraged them from thinking in terms of time. "It is not for you," He said, "to know the times or dates the Father has set by his own authority."[4] It was for them to concentrate on doing the work that needs to be done before the Second Advent can take place.

The disciples were right in associating the return of Jesus with the setting up of Christ's eternal kingdom. When Jesus comes the second time, He will come in glory and will destroy this world of sin and suffering. Peter described the events that will take place at that time in vivid terms: "That day will bring about the destruction of the heavens by fire, and the elements will melt in the heat." And again: "The heavens will disappear with a roar; the elements will be destroyed by fire, and the earth and everything in it will be laid bare."[5] But the destruction of this earth will mean its purification, and in its place there will be "a new heaven and a new earth, the home of righteousness."[6]

The church on earth at the present time is a pilgrim church. It has temporary quarters. It cannot rest satisfied with an environment of sin. It cannot be happy with sickness and suffering, with lack of harmony and cross-purposes, with human frailty and death. It must look forward to a better future, and although there is much to be thankful for in God's grace here on earth, the best is yet to come. The church looks with anticipation to the future. It prays that the church in conflict now will be the church triumphant then.

Every day the Christian prays: "Your kingdom come, your will be done on earth as it is in heaven."[7] He takes courage in the fulfillment of that prayer as seen in vision by John the revelator: "After this I looked and there before me was a great multitude that no one could count, from every nation, tribe, people and language, standing before the throne and in front of the Lamb. They were wearing white robes and were holding palm branches in their hands. And they cried out in a loud voice: 'Salvation belongs to our God, who sits on the throne, and to the Lamb.' "[8] The saints will hunger no more or feel the pangs of thirst. The Lamb will shepherd them, and God will wipe away every tear from their eyes.

But before that glorious future can come, we have duties to perform, tasks to fulfill, and conditions to meet. In this chapter we look at the church as it speeds the Second Advent.

### Wise and Foolish

One might suppose that the church consists only of perfect people, that the foolish ones are in the world, and that the saints are wise for salvation through faith in Christ Jesus. But Jesus said that at the close of earth's history the kingdom of heaven, that is, the church, will be like "ten virgins who took their lamps and went out to meet the bridegroom. Five of them were foolish and five were wise."[9]

We need not suppose that the proportion given here is exact. Fifty percent foolish is a high percentage! In what respect were they foolish? Not that they had no lamps. Not that their lamps were without oil. But that they had not taken extra oil in case of an emergency. They were not prepared for the consequences of a delay.

It was not because the foolish virgins had slept that they were called foolish. The wise virgins had slept too. Some aspects of human nature are excusable. But it is inexcusable to neglect making adequate preparation, to assume that things will go only one way. The wise are not caught by surprise. The change of schedule does not upset them. Let the bridegroom come at any time, and they are ready.

The bridegroom in the parable represents Christ. The time of His coming is not announced until the last minute. For this reason His coming has been likened to that of a thief.[10] Hence one must be ready at any moment. The oil represents the Holy Spirit.[11] The foolish virgins had not yielded their lives fully to the workings of the Holy Spirit. They may have had reservations in their dedication. Or they may not have lived up to the light that they had received.[12] In the life of the church you are either a member in the full sense of the term, or you are not a member. There is no halfway position. We cannot tell who is and who is not a member, but the truth will be revealed at the Second Coming, for some will be ready and some will not.

The suddenness of the Second Coming should not catch God's people unawares. The delay in the coming is not to make things awkward for some people. Peter made this clear when he wrote: "The Lord is not slow in keeping his promise, as some understand slowness. He is patient with you, not wanting anyone to perish, but everyone to come to repentance."[13]

Scoffers may question God's fulfillment of His promises, based on their understanding of science. Some Christians may grow lax in their spiritual perception because of their misunderstanding of prophecy. But the Second Advent is as sure as God Himself, and the church must never cease to be vigilant and ready.

### A Living Hope

Alexander Pope has said: "Hope springs eternal in the human breast;/Man never is, but always to be blest."

Every human being experiences the emotion of hope. "Better luck next time," he says to himself. As he sows his seed in the ground, he hopes for a good harvest.

But the Christian hope is based on more than wishful thinking. It is based on the goodness of God. It is based on what God has done and will do for man. It is based on God's promises.

The Christian hope is thus closely linked with faith in God and the concept of God's love. Paul said that three virtues remain: "Faith, hope and love."[14] Faith in God makes hope possible, and the love of God makes faith inevitable. While love "compels us,"[15] faith saves us,[16] and hope makes a life of hardship worth living.

Writing to the Romans, Paul pointed out that the Christian often has to endure suffering. In fact, the whole of creation is held in a kind of bondage. There is only one redeeming aspect—the condition will not last forever. There is a future glory that is worth waiting and hoping for, and "in this hope we were saved."[17] Hope makes the Christian patient while he looks forward to the future.

Peter spoke of having "a living hope through the resurrection of Jesus Christ from the dead."[18] *Living* is a favorite adjective of Peter's. Later on he referred to the "living and enduring word of God"[19] and to Christ "the living Stone" and to the members of the church as "living stones."[20] For him, everything that has to do with salvation vibrates with life. Do we see in this attitude the experience of Peter who had denied his Lord and lost all hope of being accepted back, and yet who was graciously received, commissioned, and empowered to be an apostle of Jesus Christ? The change brought him a new life and a living hope.

For Paul the "blessed hope" was "the glorious appearing of our great God and Savior, Jesus Christ."[21] He called it a blessed hope because the One who is coming again is the same One "who gave himself for us to redeem us from all wickedness and to purify for himself a people that are his very own, eager to do what is good."[22] The Christian hope was not only something that caused Paul to look forward to the future with anticipation, but it reminded him of what God had done and was doing for him.

John emphasized that we are now the children of God and that at the Second Advent "we shall be like him, for we shall see him as he is." Then he added if we have this hope in us, we shall purify ourselves, "just as he is pure."[23] Hope not only looks forward to changes that will take place in the future but catalyzes changes that need to take place now.

No wonder Christian hope is an important ingredient of Christian experience.

### Heroes of Faith

The Book of Hebrews lists those who in ancient times were heroes of the faith. It makes clear that faith has two important facets: (1) It is an assurance in one's head and heart that what God has promised and what the Christian hopes for will be fulfilled. (2) It is a recognition that the supernatural which is not necessarily evident to the physical senses is nevertheless real and is the ultimate reality.

This kind of faith is basic: (1) If we do not believe that God is, how can we come to Him? And (2) if we do not believe that He will respond favorably to our search for Him and reveal Himself to us, what is the use of trying to approach Him? Only with this kind of faith and appropriate related action can man enter a pleasing and satisfying relationship with God.[24]

This, then, is what Christian faith is all about. It begins with an implicit trust in God. It ends in doing God's will and pleasing Him.

Notice how this faith was put into practice:

1. Abel worshiped God according to God's requirements, and so God accepted his worship.

2. Enoch walked with God at a time when many denied God by their sinful actions, but Enoch knew his God by personal experience—an undeniably real experience.

3. Noah built an ark because God told him to do so, although the act seemed to have no reasonable or scientific basis.

4. Abraham followed God's instructions, preferring to be a citizen of God's kingdom rather than receiving an earthly inheritance.

5. Abraham believed that with God all things are possible, and he acted accordingly. Hence he is the father of the faithful. Many have followed in his footsteps.

In the last days of earth's history the members of the church will be men of faith. They will believe in what God has revealed and will not be carried away by science falsely so called. Peter described those who would deny the possibility of anything happening outside the realm of nature. They point to the laws of nature, which they claim are uniformitarian and immutable. But Peter also pointed out that they fell into error because they denied God's creative act as described in Genesis.[25]

The Christian is sure of his salvation because he is sure of God.

He is sure of his doctrine because he is sure of God's revelation. His faith and a hope serve as "an anchor for the soul, firm and secure."[26] Thus he is not torn or driven about by every wind of doctrine. He is secure in Christ, and he is the source of confidence for others.

## Life After Death

Death is an enemy that takes away the lives of our loved ones while we stand helplessly by. We cannot stem the tide of death. We cannot prevent the course of old age and deterioration. We never cease to feel the sting of death, although most of us try to avoid death as long as possible.

But death, real death, is a defeated enemy. When Christ broke the portals of the tomb, He proclaimed the possibility of a resurrection for all His followers. Death for the Christian is nothing more than a sleep. Jesus proclaimed, "I am the resurrection and the life."[27] When Jesus called Lazarus to come out of the tomb, he came out. And thus it will be for all the dead in Christ at the Second Advent.

Paul did not want the Thessalonians to grieve over their dead as the heathen did. The heathen might have an excuse for mourning heavily, since for them death meant the end of the road. They had no hope of a resurrection and a reunion. But for the Christian the matter was different. Death was only a sleep out of which Jesus would awaken the loved one. One had merely to wait for the resurrection at the second coming of Jesus.[28]

Some people in Corinth questioned the possibility of a resurrection, even as some people do today. But Paul pointed out that the resurrection of Christ Himself provided evidence of the possibility of a resurrection for His disciples. Can anyone doubt that Jesus was raised from the dead? Yes, some deny it. But the evidence of the Gospels is incontrovertible. It is impossible to explain the change that took place in the disciples after Easter Sunday except in terms of a real and verified risen Lord. There were too many witnesses for the matter to be seriously doubted, and the Christian faith was spread in spite of skepticism and denial.

Paul said to the Corinthians with all the conviction of faith that he could command: "Listen, I tell you a mystery: We will not all sleep, but we will all be changed—in a flash, in the twinkling of an eye, at the last trumpet. For the trumpet will sound, the dead will be raised imperishable, and we will be changed. For the perishable must clothe itself with the imperishable, and the mortal with immortality."[29]

Here is good news for every Christian. Here is a hope that one can cherish. Death will still be painful, but it will have no sting because death has been swallowed up in victory. Christians will feel with one another, but they will also be able to comfort one another.

Paul closed his appeal to the Corinthians with these words: "Therefore, my dear brothers, stand firm. Let nothing move you. Always give yourselves fully to the work of the Lord, because you know that your labor in the Lord is not in vain."[30]

## A Wedding Supper

The events that take place at the Second Advent and beyond are likened to a banquet occasion when two people are to be married and when all the relatives and friends rejoice. In what sense can the events at the Second Advent resemble a wedding reception?

A hint of the imagery comes from the parable of the ten virgins. They wait for the bridegroom to come. When the bridegroom comes, although somewhat later than expected, those who are ready go in with him to the wedding banquet.[31] Those who are not ready are shut out and cannot gain entrance. Jesus summed up the moral of the parable with the exhortation to "keep watch, because you do not know the day or the hour."[32] Those who would like to enter the festivities associated with the Second Advent must make the necessary preparations in order to be qualified to do so.

Paul also used this imagery when he wrote to the Corinthian church: "I am jealous for you with a godly jealousy. I promised you to one husband, to Christ, so that I might present you as a pure virgin to him."[33] Paul likened the church to the bride of Christ. Consequently it must be a pure bride, faithful and wholly dedicated to Christ, as a dutiful wife to a wonderful husband.

John the Baptist used similar imagery when he learned that Jesus was gaining more disciples than he. "The bride," he said, "belongs to the bridegroom."[34] He seems to have meant that the only kind of allegiance anyone can have is to Christ. He is rightly thought of as the Bridegroom. People should follow Him, not anyone else.

The Book of Revelation makes a direct relationship between the bride and the saints. " 'His bride has made herself ready. Fine linen, bright and clean, was given her to wear.' (Fine linen stands for the righteous acts of the saints.)"[35] Obviously the saints are ready for the marriage because of their righteous character. The time of the marriage is also indicated. "Hallelujah! For our Lord God Almighty reigns."[36] The time has come when the universe recognizes God's sole authority and rule. "Let us rejoice and be glad and give him glory! For the wedding of the Lamb has come."[37]

The angel added: "Blessed are those who are invited to the wedding supper of the Lamb! . . . These are the true words of God."[38]

This reminds us of the parable Jesus told about the wedding banquet.[39] Those whom the king had invited did not come to it. The Jews had heard the invitation from Jesus Himself, but they did not accept Him. They heard it a second time when the disciples spoke after Pentecost in the power of the Holy Spirit. But once again, many refused to accept the invitation. Now the gospel invitation goes to the Gentiles and to the whole world. But although the invitation goes out to all, only those who have on the wedding garment can enjoy the marriage feast. The acceptance of a wedding invitation implies adequate preparation on the part of those who accept the call.

### The New Jerusalem

We have seen that the saints constitute the bride of Christ. Scripture advises them to be ready for the wedding supper. A wedding is always an important occasion, and the bride makes all the necessary preparations so that she can be acceptable to the bridegroom. The figure of speech impresses itself upon our minds because it comes so close to human experience.

Every wedding should bring home to us the various aspects of the relationship between Christ and the church: the privilege of marrying such a wonderful husband, the thrill of receiving the love of such a perfect bridegroom, the shared joy of all the family, the beauty of the occasion when the bride is at her best, the climax of an event long kept in mind. Here is love fulfilled, communion established, and a life of happiness ever after.

But the Book of Revelation introduces us to a new concept. The angel said: "Come, I will show you the bride, the wife of the Lamb." Immediately John was carried away "to a mountain great and high," and he saw "the Holy City, Jerusalem, coming down out of heaven from God."[40]

The New Jerusalem is the capital of the new kingdom Jesus has come to establish. John saw it as part of the new heaven and new earth that replaced the first heaven and the first earth.[41] The city is "prepared as a bride beautifully dressed for her husband."[42] God now dwells with men, and they with Him. The old conditions of pain and suffering have passed away. Now there is joy forevermore.

The multiplicity of images used for the church and Christ indicates the complexity, or perhaps more exactly, the uniqueness of the relationship. Nothing on earth can compare with that which is heavenly. We can begin to grasp the meaning only as we look at it from various angles. The images used must not confuse us, but they must point up the blessedness of the relationship and the privileges that we can enjoy.

Isaiah described the calm and peace that will exist in the earth made new. He contrasted what exists in the world now with conditions to come. The wolf will live peacefully with the lamb, the leopard with the goat, the calf with the lion, the cow with the bear, and the child with the cobra or on the viper's nest. "They will neither harm nor destroy on all my holy mountain, for the earth will be full of the knowledge of the Lord, as the waters cover the sea."[43]

The church militant will become the church victorious. A pilgrim people now will be an established people then. Faith will become sight, and hope a reality. There will be no crying, no sorrow of any kind, because sin will be destroyed and the author of all lying will be cast into the lake of fire. Death will not lift up its head again. "One reminder alone remains: Our Redeemer will ever bear the marks of His crucifixion. Upon His wounded head, upon His side, His hands and feet, are the only traces of the cruel work that sin has wrought."[44]

In view of such a glorious future, what do you think we ought to be doing now?

## Footnotes

1. John 14:1-3
2. John 14:3
3. Acts 1:6
4. Acts 1:7
5. 2 Peter 3:12, 10
6. 2 Peter 3:13
7. Matthew 6:10
8. Revelation 7:9, 10
9. Matthew 25:1, 2
10. Matthew 24:42-44
11. cf. Zechariah 4
12. cf. John 8:12 and Matthew 8:11, 12
13. 2 Peter 3:9
14. 1 Corinthians 13:13
15. 2 Corinthians 5:14
16. Ephesians 2:8
17. Romans 8:18-24
18. 1 Peter 1:3
19. 1 Peter 1:23
20. 1 Peter 2:4, 5
21. Titus 2:13
22. Titus 2:14
23. 1 John 3:2, 3
24. Hebrews 11:1, 6
25. 2 Peter 3:4-7
26. Hebrews 6:19
27. John 11:25
28. 1 Thessalonians 4:13-18
29. 1 Corinthians 15:51-53
30. 1 Corinthians 15:58
31. Matthew 25:10
32. Matthew 25:13
33. 2 Corinthians 11:2
34. John 3:29
35. Revelation 19:7, 8
36. Revelation 19:6
37. Revelation 19:7
38. Revelation 19:9
39. Matthew 22:1-14
40. Revelation 21:9, 10
41. Revelation 21:1-3
42. Revelation 21:2
43. Isaiah 11:9
44. White, E. G., *The Great Controversy*, p. 674.